The Power of the Mirror

Seeing Yourself Whole in a World of Lies

Prophetess Dr. Racheal Odoy

Copyright 2026 Prophetess Dr. Racheal Odoy

Giant Publishing Company
Post Office Box 6455
Lincoln, NE 68506
www.giantpublishingcompany.com

Printed in the United States of America.

All rights reserved. No part of this publication may be used or reproduced in any form or by any means, electronic or mechanical, including photocopying, recording, or by any information storage and retrieval system, without prior written permission from the author, except for brief quotations used in reviews or articles.

Scripture quotations are from the King James Version (KJV) of the Holy Bible unless otherwise specified.

This book is a work of faith-based teaching and personal reflection. While it offers spiritual insight and encouragement, it is not intended as a substitute for professional counseling, medical advice, or legal guidance.

ISBN: 979-8-9898098-5-1
Odoy, Racheal
The Power of the Mirror
Non-fiction/Racheal Odoy
1. Non-fiction - Christianity
2. Christian living
3. Self-help

Cover design: Prophetess Dr. Racheal Odoy

Also by Prophetess Dr. Racheal Odoy:

You Need a Jonathan
Copyright 2018

I and My Seed will Thrive
Copyright 2019

You Have No Carbon Copy
Copyright 2020

Arise, Woman of Light
Copyright 2025

The Kiss of Death
Copyright 2025

Dedication

This book is dedicated to my husband, whose strength, patience, and steadfast love have been a covering through seasons both seen and unseen.

To my children - you are living reminders that restoration is possible, that renewal unfolds in time, and that beauty can emerge even after challenge. Your lives reflect promise, purpose, and hope for the future.

Above all, this work honors the gentle presence of truth - the quiet voice that reveals who we are when doubt steps in, restores clarity when the mirror is blurred, and leads us back to what is true without condemnation.

And to those healing quietly - those who smile publicly while mending privately - this book is for you. May these pages remind you that what broke you did not define you, what delayed you did not disqualify you, and what wounded you did not erase the image in which you were formed. You are seen. You are remembered. And your restoration has already begun.

Acknowledgements

I acknowledge God, in whose image we were created, and whose truth remains the original reference point by which identity finds clarity. It is His breath that gives life, His truth that restores vision, and His grace that patiently reshapes us when life distorts how we see ourselves.

I honor the Holy Spirit - the faithful teacher and gentle guide - who reveals truth quietly, corrects without condemnation, and restores clarity when doubt clouds the heart. This work exists because of His guidance, His quiet promptings, and His commitment to what is true.

I am deeply grateful for my family, whose love, sacrifice, and patience made space for this work to be birthed. Your support has been a covering, and your presence a reminder that purpose is always sustained by community.

I also acknowledge every reader who has walked through seasons of confusion, delay, disappointment, or silent struggle. Your courage to keep moving forward - even when clarity felt distant - matters more than you know. This book was written with you in mind.

Introduction - When the Mirror Stops Telling the Truth

There comes a moment in life when the mirror no longer reflects truth. You look at yourself and see limitation, while something deeper insists there is more. You see delay, while purpose quietly continues to form. You see wounds, while wisdom is being shaped beneath the surface.

The problem is not that truth has disappeared. The problem is that the mirror has begun reflecting voices it was never meant to carry.

Life leaves fingerprints on identity. Words spoken too early. Silence that lingered too long. Rejection that cut deeper than expected. Disappointment that quietly settled into the heart. Over time, these experiences begin to influence perception. What starts as reflection slowly becomes conclusion. And once reflection becomes conclusion, direction is affected.

Many people are not living beneath their potential because they lack ability or desire. They are living beneath it because they have accepted an image of themselves that was shaped by experience rather than truth. When identity becomes distorted, confidence weakens. Vision narrows. Purpose feels postponed - not because life is against us, but because clarity has been compromised.

Yet there is an original reference point for identity - one that existed before experience, failure, trauma, or opinion. Scripture describes it simply: *"So God created man in his own image." Genesis 1:27*

This means identity did not originate in circumstance. It originated in intention. Anything that contradicts that original design is not truth - it is interference.

This book is not an attempt to motivate you into becoming someone else. It is an invitation to return to who you were before life spoke louder than truth. Before disappointment named you. Before fear framed your reflection. Before comparison rewrote your value.

For those who understand life through a spiritual lens, the Holy Spirit plays a quiet but essential role in this journey. He does not force identity into place; He reveals it. When doubt steps in, clarity is gently restored. When confusion clouds vision, the mirror is cleared without condemnation. Restoration, after all, is not about creating something new; it is about uncovering what has always been true.

Throughout these pages, you will encounter Scripture, not as instruction alone, but as reflection. You will meet biblical lives that wrestled with identity, endured distortion, and emerged with clarity. You will encounter prayers that honor process rather than rush healing. And you will be invited, gently but honestly, to examine the agreements you have made with images that were never meant to define you.

This is not a book to skim. It is a mirror to sit with.

As you read, something may begin to shift. You may recognize thought patterns you never realized were shaping your decisions. You may grieve versions of yourself formed by survival rather than truth. You may experience resistance, discomfort, or release. All of it is part of restoration.

The goal is not that you admire what you see - it is that you recognize it. Because when identity is restored, movement becomes natural. Confidence becomes quiet. Purpose becomes clear.

The mirror will speak again. And this time, it will reflect truth.

The Mirror's Truth

I stood before the mirror and asked it who I was.
It answered with memories, with scars I did not invite,
with names I did not choose.

It showed me where I broke, but not where I survived. It reflected what I lost, yet missed what was preserved.

Then Truth stepped closer and gently moved the glass. I saw hands that formed me,
breath that awakened me, and a voice that said, *"This is My image."*

I am not what happened to me. I am not what they said. I am not the season that tried to erase me.
I am who God remembers. I am who truth reflects.
And now, I see.

Table of Contents

Dedication
Acknowledgments
Introduction
Poem – *The Mirror's Truth*

Chapter One   **Page**
The Reflection You Learned to Believe   **1**
- When Identity Is Taught, Not Discovered
- The Formation of an Inner Mirror
- The First Agreement You Didn't Know You Made
- Why a Distorted Reflection Is So Dangerous
- The Gentle Ministry of the Holy Spirit
- Returning to the Original Image
- *Prayer: Restoring the Reflection*

Chapter Two   **Page**
The Image Before the Injury   **17**
- Before Anything Happened to You, Something Was Already Spoken
- Creation Was Established by Speech, Not Circumstance
- You Were Spoken Into Being
- Speech Precedes Assignment

- Why the Beginning Is Always God's Reference Point
- Injury Is an Interruption, Not an Origin
- When Injury Introduces a New Lens
- Why Fear Rewrites Expectation
- Delay Does Not Cancel Calling
- How the Holy Spirit Corrects the Lens
- Recovering the Original Image
- *Prayer: Returning to the Original Image*

Chapter Three   **Page**
When the Past Tries to Name You   **43**

- The Voice That Refuses to Stay Silent
- How Memory Transforms into Authority
- When the Past Speaks Louder Than God's Promise
- Joseph: Redefining the Narrative
- Forgiveness: The Moment the Past Loses Its Authority
- God's Pattern of Renaming
- Abram: From History to Promise
- Jacob: From Survival to Authority
- Simon: From Instability to Assignment
- What Renaming Reveals about God
- When God Names You, the Past Must Be Silent
- What Name Have You Been Answering To?
- *Prayer: Releasing Old Names*

Chapter Four   **Page**
Breaking Agreement with False Images   **69**
- The Quiet Power of Agreement
- How False Images Are Formed
- Gideon: When Fear Shapes Identity
- False Images Resist Truth
- The Role of the Word in Breaking Agreement
- Replacing Agreement, Not Just Removing It
- Guarding New Agreements
- Choosing Alignment Over Familiarity
- What Are You Still Agreeing With?
- *Prayer: Releasing and Replacing Agreements*

Chapter Five   **Page**
The Word of God as the True Mirror   **91**
- Why Every Other Mirror Eventually Fails
- The Word Reveals Without Wounding
- Why Circumstances Make a Poor Mirror
- David: Recalibrating the Soul with the Word
- Jesus: Living from the Word as Identity
- How the Word Corrects Inner Narratives
- Living Daily from the True Mirror
- Which Mirror Are You Using?
- *Prayer: Living from the True Mirror*

Chapter Six   **Page**
When Comparison Distorts the Mirror   **109**

- The Subtle Theft of Identity
- Why Comparison Feels So Convincing
- Saul and David: When Comparison Turns Destructive
- Comparison Weakens Gratitude and Distorts Timing
- The Illusion of Equal Timelines
- Returning the Mirror to God
- Living Free from the Comparison Trap
- Where Has Comparison Been Speaking?
- *Prayer: Releasing Comparison*

Chapter Seven   **Page**
The Role of Faith: Seeing Beyond What Is   127

- Faith Begins Where Sight Ends
- Seeing Through God's Perspective
- Abraham: Trusting Beyond Evidence
- Faith Sustains Identity During Delay
- Peter: Learning to See Beyond the Storm
- Faith Is Built Through the Word
- Faith Produces Movement, Not Passivity
- Living by Faith Daily
- *Prayer: Strengthening Spiritual Sight*

Chapter Eight   **Page**
God's Plan vs. Man's Plans   143

- Life Is Always Being Directed by a Plan

- Personal Plans: Desire, Fear, and Control
- Family and Generational Plans
- Community and Cultural Influence
- Friends and Familiar Voices
- The Enemy's Plan: Distraction and Distortion
- God's Plan: Eternal, Redemptive, and Precise
- Yielding Without Losing Hope
- Whose Plan is Guiding Your Direction?
- *Prayer: Surrendering Competing Plans*

Chapter Nine   **Page**
From Reflection to Revelation   **157**
- When Seeing Turns Into Knowing
- Why Reflection Alone Can Leave You Stuck
- Peter: When Revelation Redefines Identity
- The Holy Spirit: Interpreter of Meaning
- When Revelation Reignites Direction
- Revelation Brings Peace Before Details
- From Revelation to Obedience
- Living Revealed, Not Confused
- *Prayer: Walking in Revelation*

Chapter Ten   **Page**
Walking in Alignment   **173**
- Alignment Is a Daily Posture, Not a One-Time Decision
- Ordering Your Life Around Revelation

- Walking in the Spirit: The Key to Sustained Alignment
- Alignment Produces Inner Peace
- Consistency Over Intensity
- Correction Is Part of Alignment
- Remaining Aligned in Uncertain Seasons
- Alignment Requires Ongoing Surrender
- *Prayer: Walking in Alignment*

Chapter Eleven   **Page**
Guarding the Image You Now See   **191**
- Clarity Must Be Protected
- Why the Enemy Targets Identity After Revelation
- Renewing the Mind to Preserve the Image
- Guarding Your Words
- Choosing Environment Wisely
- Jesus: Guarding Identity in the Wilderness
- Rest as a Guardrail
- Staying Submitted to the Holy Spirit
- *Prayer: Guarding What God Has Restored*

Chapter Twelve   **Page**
Living from the True Image   **215**
- From Protection to Expression
- Identity as a Foundation, Not a Question
- Living Authentically Without Apology

- Authority Flows from Identity
- Living from Rest, Not Striving
- Becoming a Living Reflection
- *Prayer: Living from the True Image*

Chapter Thirteen   **Page**
Leaving the Old Image Behind   **233**
- Release Is Required for Permanence
- Why the Old Image Tries to Follow You
- The Danger of Keeping Old Labels
- Lot's Wife: When the Old Image Is Not Released
- Leaving Without Resentment
- Agreeing Fully with Who God Says You Are
- Living Forward Without Negotiation
- *Prayer: Releasing the Old Image*

Chapter Fourteen   **Page**
Established in the Image   **249**
- From Transformation to Permanence
- When Identity No Longer Wavers
- Living Established, Not Defensive
- Established Faith Produces Endurance
- Established to Reflect Christ Consistently
- A Life That Does Not Return
- *Prayer: Established in the Image*

A Final Word to the Reader
A Sealing Prayer for You

Chapter One
The Reflection You Learned to Believe

When Identity Is Taught, Not Discovered

No one is born questioning their worth. Doubt is not native to the human spirit—it is introduced. Identity confusion does not arrive suddenly; it is learned quietly through repetition, exposure, and survival. Long before a person has language for fear or insecurity, they are already absorbing information about who they are and how they are received.

Before you ever named fear, it learned your environment. Before insecurity spoke, it was modeled. Before self-doubt felt personal, it was planted.

Identity is first learned through observation, not instruction. Children watch how presence is received, how mistakes are handled, how emotions are responded to, and how silence is used. They learn whether they are safe to be seen, whether they must perform to be accepted, or whether parts of themselves should be hidden to remain secure. These lessons are rarely spoken aloud, yet they are deeply formative.

Life becomes a classroom, and identity becomes the lesson—taught by tone, reaction, absence, correction, rejection, and sometimes love that did not know how to speak clearly. Even well-meaning environments can transmit distorted reflections when affirmation is inconsistent or clarity is missing. Over time, the soul begins to gather conclusions about what is required to belong, to be valued, or to be safe.

These conclusions are rarely intentional, but they are powerful. They settle beneath conscious thought and begin to guide behavior. A person may not remember when they learned to shrink, to strive, to stay quiet, or to overachieve—but the pattern remains. What was once an adaptation slowly becomes an identity.

You begin to live according to what reflection allows. You move where you feel permitted. You hesitate where confidence was never affirmed. You adjust your expression to match what you learned would be accepted.

This is how identity becomes taught rather than discovered—not through one defining moment, but through many quiet ones. And what is learned over time often feels personal, even when it was never original.

This chapter begins the process of separating what you learned from who you are—so that identity can move from survival back to truth.

The Formation of an Inner Mirror
Every human being carries an inner mirror—a place where self-perception forms. That mirror was designed to reflect God's image, but life often rearranges its surface. What was meant to reflect truth becomes shaped by experience, and clarity slowly gives way to interpretation.

Words spoken over you became etchings. Repeated statements—whether affirming or critical—left impressions. Even words spoken casually, emotionally, or without intention settled into the mirror over time. What was said once may have stung, but what was said often began to define.

Experiences became frames. Moments of success, failure, rejection, or approval created boundaries around how you learned to see yourself. Experiences did not merely happen to you; they taught you what to expect. They framed what felt possible, what felt risky, and what felt out of reach. Over time, the frame became familiar, even when it was limiting.

Pain became a filter. Unresolved pain does not remain neutral. It colors perception. It influences interpretation. When pain is present, the mirror no longer reflects clearly; it filters what is seen. Innocent interactions are viewed cautiously. Opportunity feels uncertain. Trust becomes selective. The mirror begins to reflect not what *is*, but what has *hurt*.

What you repeatedly heard, you eventually believed. What you consistently experienced, you learned to expect. What you survived, you adapted to.

This is not weakness—it is human nature. Adaptation is a form of protection. It allows the soul to endure environments it did not choose. But when adaptation becomes permanent, it quietly reshapes identity. Adaptation, when left unchecked, becomes distortion. What once helped you survive can later limit how you live. The mirror no longer reflects truth; it reflects what was necessary at the time.

Scripture reminds us that identity was never meant to be externally sourced: *"So God created man in his own image, in the image of God created he him."* Genesis 1:27

That means identity preceded experience. Reflection came before reaction. Truth existed before trauma.

The mirror was never designed to learn who you are from life. It was designed to remember who you were from the beginning. This is why restoration is possible. The image was not lost—it was covered. And what was covered can be revealed again.

The First Agreement You Didn't Know You Made

The most dangerous agreements are not spoken aloud; they are settled inwardly. They do not announce themselves as beliefs. They form quietly, often during moments when understanding is limited and protection feels necessary. These agreements are rarely chosen—they are concluded.

I must not be enough.
I have to try harder to be accepted.
I will always struggle.
I am behind.
I missed it.

These thoughts feel personal, but they are learned responses to distorted mirrors. They are conclusions drawn from repetition, disappointment, or absence—not from truth. Over time, they stop sounding like thoughts and begin sounding like facts.

Once accepted, these agreements quietly shape decisions. They influence how you enter rooms, how you respond to opportunity, how you interpret silence, and how you measure progress. You begin to shrink where you were meant to stand. You hesitate where you were meant to advance. You explain yourself where you were meant to rest.

The power of these agreements lies in their subtlety. They do not demand attention; they assume authority. They influence choices without asking permission. A person may believe they are making logical decisions, when in reality they are protecting an agreement that was never meant to govern identity.

Identity does not collapse loudly—it erodes silently.

Scripture gives us a clear picture of this progression in the garden. Adam's response reveals how quickly perception can shift once an agreement is made.

"And he said, I heard thy voice in the garden, and I was afraid, because I was naked; and I hid myself." Genesis 3:10

Adam did not hide because God rejected him. He hid because his reflection changed. Something happened internally before anything changed externally. Shame introduced a new way of seeing himself, and behavior followed perception.

Nothing about Adam's design had changed. Nothing about God's presence had shifted. What changed was the agreement Adam made about what his nakedness now meant. Shame always alters identity before it alters action.

This is how the first agreement works. It redefines meaning. It takes something neutral—or even good—and assigns it a false interpretation. Innocence becomes exposure. Silence becomes rejection. Delay becomes failure. Over time, the soul begins responding to life through agreements that were never spoken by God. These agreements feel protective, but they are limiting. They may have helped you survive a season, but they cannot lead you into wholeness. What was learned in response to pain cannot remain in authority once truth is revealed.

This chapter invites awareness—not accusation. You are not at fault for what you learned in moments of vulnerability. But awareness creates responsibility. What was unconsciously agreed with can now be consciously released.

The work of restoration begins here—not by fighting behavior, but by uncovering agreements. When false agreements lose their authority, identity begins to stabilize. The mirror starts to clear. And clarity becomes possible again.

Why a Distorted Reflection Is So Dangerous
A distorted reflection is dangerous not because it is dramatic, but because it is subtle. It does not usually announce itself as falsehood; it presents itself as wisdom, caution, or realism. Over time, it begins to feel responsible—even protective.

Opposition does not need to stop your destiny if identity is confused. It does not need to close doors if hesitation develops at open ones. It does not need to create failure if uncertainty is accepted as truth.

When reflection is distorted, courage weakens quietly. A person may still believe in God, still desire purpose, still pray for direction—yet live cautiously. Not because opportunity is absent, but because confidence has been compromised. The soul begins to question whether movement is safe, deserved, or sustainable.

A distorted reflection produces inconsistent confidence, delayed obedience, compromised authority, and negotiated purpose. Confidence becomes situational rather than steady. Obedience becomes conditional rather than responsive. Authority is present, but unused. Purpose is acknowledged, but postponed.

These patterns rarely feel spiritual. They feel practical. They sound like patience, humility, or discernment. But beneath them is often an unexamined belief: *I am not ready yet. I am not enough yet. I will move when I am more secure.* Scripture warns us of this subtle danger: *"As he thinketh in his heart, so is he."* Proverbs 23:7

When thinking shifts, being follows. Life eventually aligns with perception. A distorted inner mirror does not simply affect how you feel—it affects how you choose, how you wait, and how you respond when God invites movement.

This is why identity confusion is more dangerous than external resistance. External opposition can be confronted. Circumstances can be challenged. But internal distortion quietly governs behavior without confrontation. It shapes limits that God never placed. A person with a distorted reflection may stand before opportunity and feel unqualified, even when equipped. They may hear invitation and interpret it as pressure. They may sense calling and respond with delay. Not because they are disobedient, but because their reflection no longer supports courage.

Distortion also affects authority. Authority flows most freely when identity is settled. When identity is unclear, authority feels risky. The believer hesitates to speak, to lead, to decide, or to stand firmly—fearing exposure, rejection, or failure. Authority becomes something to manage rather than something to exercise.

Yet Scripture consistently ties authority to identity, not performance. When identity is clear, obedience becomes simpler. Courage becomes quieter. Decisions become less reactive.

This is why restoration must address reflection, not just behavior. Correcting actions without correcting identity only creates temporary change. But when the mirror is clarified, behavior begins to align naturally.

Distortion is dangerous because it convinces the soul to live beneath what was already given. It does not remove calling—it delays expression. It does not erase purpose—it negotiates it.

This chapter is not meant to create urgency through fear. It is meant to create clarity through understanding. When the danger is named, it loses power. When distortion is recognized, it can be corrected. And when reflection is restored, courage no longer feels forced. Movement becomes natural again.

The Gentle Ministry of the Holy Spirit
Restoration does not begin with force; it begins with revelation. Identity is not repaired through pressure or self-correction. It is restored through clarity—when truth is remembered rather than demanded.

Many people assume change must be loud to be effective. Yet the most lasting transformations are often quiet. They occur when understanding settles rather than when emotion spikes. Restoration begins when something within you recognizes what has always been true.

For those who understand life through a spiritual lens, the Holy Spirit serves this gentle role. He does not shout truth into existence—He reveals it. He does not accuse—He reminds. When doubt steps in, He quietly uncovers what God already established before distortion occurred. Scripture describes this ministry with care: *"But the Comforter, which is the Holy Ghost… he shall teach you all things, and bring all things to your remembrance." John 14:26*

Remembrance is holy work. Not remembering pain—but remembering origin. Not rehearsing failure—but recovering truth.

The Holy Spirit does not create a new identity. He reconnects you to the one that was already formed. He brings clarity without condemnation and conviction without shame. Layer by layer, false reflections are removed—not through confrontation, but through understanding. This is why restoration often feels gentle rather than dramatic. The Spirit works at the pace of trust. He restores sight slowly enough for the soul to remain safe, yet clearly enough for truth to become undeniable.

When identity is restored this way, it is not fragile. It does not rely on emotional highs or external validation. It becomes steady—because it has been remembered, not reconstructed.

This is the nature of true restoration. What was covered is revealed. What was forgotten is brought back into view. And clarity returns without force.

Returning to the Original Image
Your truest self predates your worst season. Before disappointment shaped your expectations, before failure influenced your confidence, before survival taught you how to adapt—you were already formed with intention. Your calling existed before your confusion. Your worth was never negotiated by failure.

Identity was not something you earned over time; it was something you were given from the beginning. Life may have added layers, interpretations, and conclusions, but it did not rewrite your original design.

God never consults your history to define your future. He consults His image. This is what makes restoration possible. The work is not about becoming someone new, but about returning to what was always true. What life distorted did not erase what God formed. What survival reshaped can be reshaped again—this time by truth.

The life of **David** illustrates this clearly. David was overlooked, underestimated, and misunderstood long before he was recognized. While others evaluated him by appearance, age, and position, God saw something deeper—something already present. *"Man looketh on the outward appearance, but the Lord looketh on the heart." 1 Samuel 16:7*

David's identity was not established when he was anointed publicly; it was recognized. God did not create something new in that moment—He revealed what had already been there. David's confidence, courage, and capacity were formed long before validation arrived.

What God sees is not distorted. He is not confused by your seasons. He is not misled by your setbacks. This is why restoration does not require self-accusation. This chapter is not an indictment—it is an invitation. An invitation to release what you learned through pressure and recover what you were given through purpose. An invitation to separate adaptation from identity, and survival from truth.

The mirror can be corrected. Not by denying what happened—but by realigning what defines you. The image can be restored. Not because you worked harder—but because it was never lost.

Returning to the original image does not erase your story; it places it in proper order. Experience becomes context, not authority. Pain becomes part of the journey, not the definition of the traveler. And when the original image is restored, movement becomes natural again. You no longer strive to become—you remember how to stand.

Prayer: Restoring the Reflection
Father,
I bring before You every image of myself shaped by pain, fear, rejection, or misunderstanding. Where I learned wrongly, teach me again. Where I accepted what was untrue, replace it with clarity and truth. By Your Holy Spirit, restore my sight. Gently reconnect me to the image You formed from the beginning—before distortion, before confusion, before survival reshaped how I see myself. I release false agreements and receive clarity, courage, and an identity rooted in what is true. I choose to live from that truth going forward. In Jesus' name, Amen.

Chapter Two
The Image Before the Injury

Before Anything Happened to You, Something Was Already Spoken Over You

Before anything happened to you, something was already spoken over you. Before your environment shaped you, you were already addressed. Before life introduced contradiction, an original intention existed. Before pain attempted to rename you, purpose had already been declared.

This is why the beginning matters. Identity is not formed by reaction; it is established by origin. Long before you learned how to survive, you were already designed for more than survival. Long before life taught you what to fear, truth had already defined what you were made to carry.

Many people try to understand themselves by starting with their experiences—what happened, what went wrong, what was said, what was lost. But Scripture begins somewhere else. It begins with God speaking first, not life speaking loudest. *"In the beginning God created the heaven and the earth." Genesis 1:1*

The beginning reveals God's method. God does not wait for conditions to improve before He speaks. He establishes order before order is visible. He introduces meaning before meaning is felt. He does not respond to chaos—He commands it. He does not negotiate with darkness—He speaks light. *"And God said, Let there be light: and there was light." Genesis 1:3*

This is more than a creation story. It is a pattern. God speaks first. His Word does not describe reality—it forms it. And in the same way, your identity was never meant to be decided by what happened to you later. It was meant to be anchored in what was spoken from the beginning.

When life becomes painful, the instinct is to start defining yourself from the injury. But God's reference point has always been earlier than the wound. He returns to what He established before distortion entered the picture. That is the heart of restoration: not inventing a new self, but recovering the original image.

Creation Was Established by Speech, Not Circumstance

The earth was without form. Darkness covered the deep. Nothing looked ordered, stable, or promising. Yet God did not consult the condition—He released His voice. *"And God said, Let there be light: and there was light." Genesis 1:3*

Creation did not improve gradually; it responded immediately. The moment God spoke, reality adjusted. Light did not struggle to appear. It did not negotiate with darkness. It did not wait for permission from circumstance. It obeyed.

This detail matters because it reveals a consistent principle: **God establishes reality by speech, not by circumstance.** Conditions may describe what is visible, but they do not determine what is possible. God did not allow the absence of light to define the future of creation. He addressed the absence with intention.

When God speaks, He is not commenting on what exists—He is creating what must exist. His words do not reflect reality; they form it.

This same principle applies to identity. Long before circumstances described who you would become, something was already spoken over you. Your identity was never meant to be shaped by the environment you were born into, the experiences you encountered, or the seasons that challenged you. Those things may have influenced perception, but they were never authorized to define essence. Circumstances describe conditions. Speech determines identity.

This is why beginning matters. God always returns to what He spoke first. He does not revise identity based on later conditions. He does not renegotiate purpose based on disruption. What He establishes by speech remains authoritative—even when the environment suggests otherwise.

Life may attempt to redefine you through experience, delay, or pain. But creation reminds us of something steady: **what is spoken with intention carries more authority than what is seen in disorder.**

When God speaks, clarity enters. When God speaks, alignment begins. When God speaks, reality reorganizes itself around truth.

Restoration, then, is not about convincing God to speak again. It is about returning to what was already spoken—and allowing life to realign around it.

You Were Spoken Into Being
When God came to humanity, His language slowed—not because He was unsure, but because identity required intention. Creation moved quickly until this point. Light, land, sky, and sea were spoken into place with command. But when it came time to create humanity, Scripture records something different: *"And God said, Let us make man in our image, after our likeness…" Genesis 1:26*

This was counsel, not impulse. Humanity was not produced in haste. God did not merely command man into existence; He **considered** him. The language reveals deliberation. Before man ever breathed, God determined how humanity would reflect, rule, and relate. Identity was decided before experience began. Creation up to this point responded to command. Humanity responded to **design**. *"So God created man in his own image, in the image of God created he him..." Genesis 1:27*

This means identity did not originate in family systems, culture, success, failure, trauma, rejection, or environment. Those influences came later. You were formed from divine likeness before you were exposed to human limitation. Before anyone evaluated you, labeled you, misunderstood you, or compared you, heaven had already affirmed you. The image was not borrowed. It was not assigned later. It was embedded at creation.

This is why injury cannot be your origin story. Injury may have altered perception, but it did not establish essence. Experience may have reshaped how you see yourself, but it did not rewrite what you were made from. The injury came later. The image came first.

This distinction matters. When people define themselves from pain, they begin at the wrong point. God never starts with what happened to you. He starts with what He formed in you. Restoration does not deny injury—it refuses to let injury become the reference point.

You were not spoken into being by circumstance. You were not shaped into existence by survival. You were spoken into being by intention. And what is spoken with intention carries permanence.

This is why healing is possible. This is why identity can be restored. Because the original image was never lost—it was simply covered.

Chapter Two continues to unfold this truth: **what God spoke first still speaks loudest**—if you know where to listen.

Speech Precedes Assignment
After identity was established, God spoke assignment. *"And God blessed them, and God said unto them, Be fruitful, and multiply, and replenish the earth, and subdue it..." Genesis 1:28*

Notice the order. God did not command effort before releasing blessing. He did not demand productivity before declaring fruitfulness. He did not assign responsibility before establishing authority. Blessing came first. Instruction followed.

This order matters because it reveals how God works with people. Assignment is never meant to create identity; it is meant to **express** it. Responsibility does not define worth; it flows from it. God spoke fruitfulness into humanity before humanity had proven anything. Authority preceded responsibility.

This reveals a truth many miss: You were empowered before you were tested.

God did not wait to see if humanity could succeed before He entrusted them with responsibility. He established capacity first. Fruitfulness was not a goal to be earned; it was a condition already declared. Assignment was not punishment; it was partnership. When this order is reversed, life becomes exhausting. People begin striving to earn what was meant to be received. They attempt to prove worth through performance, productivity, or perfection. Injury convinces people they must earn what God already spoke.

Restoration corrects this distortion. It reminds us that identity and blessing are not rewards—they are foundations. Assignment does not validate you; it **reveals** you.

When people define themselves by what they do, failure becomes devastating and success becomes fragile. But when identity is anchored first, effort becomes expression rather than pressure. Responsibility becomes meaningful rather than heavy.

God's pattern is consistent: He speaks before He sends. He blesses before He assigns. He establishes before He instructs.

This is why returning to the original image changes how life is lived. You no longer move from fear of failure, but from confidence in what has already been declared. Work becomes purposeful, not proving. Obedience becomes responsive, not anxious.

Assignment was never meant to create identity. It was meant to reveal it. And when identity is restored to its proper place, responsibility no longer feels like a burden—it feels like alignment.

Why the Beginning Is Always God's Reference Point

God never defines a life from the moment it faltered. He defines it from the moment He spoke.

Human systems tend to measure identity by outcomes—by success, failure, consistency, or reputation. But God measures identity by origin. What begins in God is not canceled by what happens in time. What He establishes at the beginning remains His reference point, even when the journey becomes complicated. Scripture makes this principle unmistakably clear: *"Known unto God are all his works from the beginning of the world." Acts 15:18*

God is never surprised by progression. He does not revise identity based on disruption. He does not redefine purpose because of delay. He does not abandon original intention when humanity stumbles. His view is anchored in what He knew, spoke, and formed from the start.

This is why failure, while serious, is never final. Failure disrupts fellowship, but it does not delete identity.

Even after sin entered the world, Scripture affirms that humanity still bore divine likeness: *"For in the image of God made he man." Genesis 9:6*

This statement comes *after* the fall. It confirms something essential: the image was not erased by disobedience. Relationship was affected. Trust was fractured. But identity remained intact. God addressed the breach—but He did not erase the image.

This pattern continues throughout Scripture. When God restores, He does not rehearse failure—He reestablishes calling.

When Jesus restored **Peter**, He did not replay the moment of denial. He did not shame Peter with a summary of his mistakes. Instead, He returned Peter to his original assignment. *"Feed my sheep." John 21:17*

Jesus restored Peter by reconnecting him to purpose, not by revisiting his lowest moment. The reference point was not denial—it was calling. Peter's failure did not redefine him; it interrupted him. Restoration brought him back to what had been spoken before fear ever entered the picture.

This is how God restores lives. He does not ask people to earn their way back into identity. He invites them to return to what was already established. He does not build futures from shame; He builds them from truth.

The beginning matters because it carries authority. What God spoke first still speaks loudest. And what He established originally remains the foundation for restoration.

When identity is rebuilt from the beginning, healing becomes steady. Shame loses its voice. Movement becomes possible again—not because the past is ignored, but because it is no longer the reference point.

God restores by reconnecting people to original purpose, not by rehashing mistakes. And when the beginning is recovered, the future regains clarity.

Injury Is an Interruption, Not an Origin
Injury feels like a beginning, but it is not. It may mark a turning point in memory, but it is not the source of identity. It is an interruption—not an origin.

Pain often convinces people that life started changing *there*. That the moment of betrayal, loss, rejection, or failure became the defining point. But interruption is not creation. Something existed before the interruption occurred. Something was already in motion before injury entered the story. This is why God consistently reminds His servants who they were **before** fear, rejection, or delay attempted to rename them.

To **Jeremiah**, God said: *"Before I formed thee in the belly I knew thee." Jeremiah 1:5*

Jeremiah's calling did not begin with his insecurity. It did not originate in his hesitation or fear. God referenced Jeremiah's identity before formation, before voice, before resistance. What came later could not undo what was already known.

To **Gideon**, hiding in fear and scarcity, God declared: *"The Lord is with thee, thou mighty man of valour." Judges 6:12*

Gideon was called mighty while still hiding. God did not wait for confidence to appear before naming strength. He addressed identity before behavior aligned. The injury of fear did not redefine Gideon—it interrupted his awareness of who he already was.

And to **David**, overlooked and unseen, God instructed Samuel: *"Arise, anoint him: for this is he." 1 Samuel 16:12*

David was chosen before the crown was visible. Before recognition. Before validation. Before evidence. God did not consult circumstance to determine calling. He identified David based on what He had already established.

Across these lives, the pattern remains consistent: God speaks identity before circumstances agree. Injury explains pain, but it does not authorize surrender. Delay explains timing, but it does not redefine purpose. Interruption explains disruption, but it does not originate identity.

What interrupted you did not create you. What wounded you did not name you. What delayed you did not disqualify you.

God always returns to what He spoke *before* the interruption—because origin carries more authority than injury. And when origin is recovered, healing begins to move forward with clarity rather than confusion.

The Image Before the Injury: When Injury Introduces a New Lens
Injury does not immediately change who you are. It changes how you see.

Pain introduces a lens—subtle at first, protective by design. It trains the heart to scan for danger, the mind to brace for disappointment, and the spirit to guard itself against hope. This lens is not created out of weakness; it is formed out of survival. It exists to help the soul endure what it did not expect. But what begins as protection can quietly become perception. Over time, this lens begins to influence interpretation. Neutral moments feel threatening. Silence feels personal. Opportunity feels risky. The heart no longer responds to what is present—it reacts to what is remembered. You stop seeing life as it is. You begin seeing life as it once hurt you.

This is how distortion takes root—not by force, but by familiarity. The lens becomes trusted because it feels safe. It feels wise. It feels realistic. Yet it is no longer neutral. It filters truth through experience instead of allowing truth to interpret experience.

Scripture offers a powerful contrast through the life of **Joseph**. Joseph experienced betrayal by those closest to him. He was sold into slavery, falsely accused, and forgotten in prison. Every external condition suggested abandonment, failure, and loss of favor. Yet Scripture repeatedly records one unchanging truth: *"And the Lord was with Joseph."* Genesis 39:2

Joseph's environment changed, but his reference point did not. He did not allow pain to become the lens through which he interpreted God's presence or his own identity. Injury touched his circumstances, but it never became his definition. Joseph did not deny what happened to him—but he refused to let it rename him.

Because Joseph did not allow pain to redefine him, pain could not detour him. His integrity remained intact. His discernment stayed sharp. His capacity to lead and interpret dreams remained active, even in confinement. What could have embittered him instead refined him—because the lens was never allowed to replace the image.

Many people are not delayed by God. They are delayed by a lens shaped by injury. When injury becomes the lens, life is interpreted through caution rather than calling. Movement feels dangerous. Trust feels expensive. Hope feels naive. The future is measured by the past rather than by promise.

Restoration begins when the lens is acknowledged but no longer obeyed. Healing does not require forgetting what happened—it requires refusing to let what happened define how you see everything else.

The image came before the injury. And when the image becomes the reference point again, clarity begins to return.

Why Fear Rewrites Expectation
Fear rarely announces itself. It does not always arrive as panic or dread. More often, it rewrites expectation quietly. Fear changes what a person anticipates. Where hope once looked forward, fear begins to brace. Where confidence once assumed possibility, fear assumes limitation. Over time, expectation shifts—not because God changed His intention, but because fear adjusted the lens through which the future is viewed. This rewriting often follows injury.

The life of **Moses** illustrates this clearly. Moses encountered leadership early. Raised in Pharaoh's house, trained in authority, exposed to governance, he carried instinctive confidence. He understood systems of power. He knew how to speak, decide, and act. But one moment of failure—followed by rejection and isolation—reshaped how he saw himself. What had once felt natural became questionable. What had once seemed possible now felt presumptuous.

Years later, when God called Moses again, Moses did not question the assignment—he questioned himself. *"Who am I, that I should go unto Pharaoh?" Exodus 3:11*

This question reveals how fear works. Moses did not doubt God's ability. He doubted his own legitimacy. Fear had rewritten expectation. Injury had narrowed vision. Leadership no longer felt natural—it felt risky. Fear does this quietly. It convinces people that what once fit them now exceeds them. It reframes calling as pressure and responsibility as exposure. The future is no longer approached with confidence, but with hesitation.

God did not correct Moses by rehearsing his past. He did not defend Moses' qualifications. He did not argue with Moses' self-assessment. Instead, God restored the reference point. *"Certainly I will be with thee." Exodus 3:12*

God's answer to distorted identity is not explanation—it is assurance. He did not say, *You are capable.* He said, *You are not alone.* Presence realigns perception.

Fear isolates the self. Presence recenters the soul.

When presence is restored, expectation shifts again. The future is no longer measured by past failure, but by present alignment. Confidence does not come from self-confidence—it comes from knowing who is with you.

This is how fear is undone. Not by force, but by presence. Not by self-correction, but by restored reference. When God becomes the reference point again, expectation widens. Vision steadies. Movement becomes possible. And the future no longer looks like a threat—it looks like obedience.

Delay Does Not Cancel Calling
Delay often feels like disqualification. When time stretches longer than expected, the heart begins to interpret waiting as rejection. Questions surface quietly: *Did I miss it? Did I wait too long? Was I wrong about what I sensed?* Yet Scripture tells a different story. Calling is not fragile. It is not undone by time, obscurity, or process. Delay does not weaken what God has spoken—it matures it.

The life of **David** reflects this clearly. David was anointed in private and returned to obscurity. Years passed between the oil and the throne. He faced misunderstanding, danger, and seasons where the promise seemed distant. Yet the delay did not cancel the calling—it prepared him for it.

David learned to trust God before ruling people. He learned to lead sheep before leading a nation. He learned to anchor his confidence in God's presence rather than in position. *"The Lord is my light and my salvation; whom shall I fear?" Psalm 27:1*

Delay refined David's dependence. It did not diminish his destiny.

Delay also does not invalidate identity after failure. The story of **Peter** makes this clear. Peter's denial was public and painful. It contradicted his own self-image as loyal and courageous. In a moment of fear, he became someone he did not recognize. Yet Jesus did not revoke Peter's assignment. He did not reduce Peter's role. He restored him through love, not shame. *"Simon, son of Jonas, lovest thou me?" John 21:15* Each question was not an interrogation—it was a restoration. And then Jesus returned Peter to purpose. *"Feed my sheep." John 21:17*

Jesus did not restore Peter to a smaller version of himself. He restored him to original calling—with greater depth, humility, and compassion. What failure interrupted did not cancel what was spoken.

Delay tests perception, not promise. Waiting reveals what the heart is anchored to. Failure exposes where identity is sourced. But none of these have authority to cancel calling.

God never restores people backward. He restores them forward—with wisdom gained, depth added, and dependence strengthened.

Delay does not mean denial. It means preparation is still in progress. And when the time comes, what God spoke will not need to be reissued. It will simply unfold.

How the Holy Spirit Corrects the Lens
The Holy Spirit does not shatter distorted lenses abruptly. He cleans them patiently. Restoration rarely comes through confrontation. It comes through illumination. The Holy Spirit restores sight without shaming the soul for what it learned while trying to survive. He understands how distortion formed, and He corrects it with care. He restores without accusation. He reveals without condemnation. He corrects without crushing.

This is why correction through the Spirit feels different from criticism. Criticism points out error and leaves the heart exposed. Correction reveals truth and leaves the heart secure. The Spirit does not demand immediate clarity; He guides the heart back to alignment at a pace that preserves trust. Scripture describes this ministry clearly: *"But the Comforter, which is the Holy Ghost… he shall teach you all things, and bring all things to your remembrance." John 14:26*

Remembrance is holy work. Not remembering pain—but remembering truth. Not revisiting wounds—but recovering what was spoken before distortion entered.

The Holy Spirit does not introduce new identity; He reintroduces original truth. When fear has trained the heart to expect loss, the Spirit reminds the soul of promise. When pain has shaped perception, He gently restores clarity. He returns the heart to what God spoke before fear learned your patterns.

This correction happens gradually. Distortion is not removed all at once, because clarity must be sustained, not forced. Layer by layer, the lens is cleaned. Assumptions are softened. Conclusions are revisited.

False agreements lose their authority—not through effort, but through understanding. Scripture describes the effect of this process: *"The entrance of thy words giveth light; it giveth understanding unto the simple." Psalm 119:130*

Light does not argue with darkness—it replaces it. Understanding does not shame confusion—it resolves it.

This is how the Holy Spirit heals perception. He does not fight what you learned; He outgrows it. He does not accuse the past; He restores the present. And as clarity returns, the heart begins to respond to life from truth rather than from memory.

When the lens is corrected this way, identity stabilizes. Fear loosens its grip. Expectation widens. Life is no longer interpreted through what once hurt—but through what is now revealed. This is not forceful change. It is faithful restoration.

Recovering the Original Image
Restoration is not replacement; it is recovery. God does not erase what was wounded, nor does He abandon what was touched by pain. He restores what was original—returning the soul to its intended

alignment rather than forcing it to become something unfamiliar.

When life injures a person, it often convinces them that they must begin again as someone else. Pain suggests reinvention. Survival encourages adjustment. But God's way is different. He does not build a new identity to replace the old one. He uncovers what was already there before injury introduced distortion. What was covered was not destroyed. What was wounded was not lost.

This is why God speaks of restoration in terms of *return*, not reinvention. *"And I will restore to you the years that the locust hath eaten." Joel 2:25*

This promise reaches far beyond time. It speaks to identity, purpose, and alignment. God does not merely restore opportunities; He restores the inner capacity to recognize and walk in them. He restores confidence where fear settled, clarity where confusion lingered, and trust where disappointment once ruled. The locust did not create you, and it does not get to define what remains.

The work of restoration belongs to the Holy Spirit. He does not arrive to manufacture a new version of you; He arrives to reveal the one God already spoke into existence. He gently removes the layers that survival added and exposes the truth that was present before pain learned your patterns. Scripture describes this work with quiet authority: *"He restoreth my soul."* Psalm 23:3

To restore the soul is to realign it with truth. It is to return the heart to its original posture—before disappointment hardened it, before fear narrowed its vision, before survival became a strategy. The soul does not need replacement; it needs remembrance. This is why healing often feels like recognition. Something within you responds—not because what you are becoming is new, but because what is being restored is familiar to heaven. Restoration awakens what was dormant, not by force, but by truth.

You are not starting over. You are returning. You are returning to the image God formed before life spoke loudly. You are returning to the identity declared before injury attempted to interrupt the narrative. What God spoke in the beginning did not expire with time, and it did not weaken with experience. What He declared before injury still speaks now.

Prayer: Returning to the Original Image
Father,
I release every lens shaped by pain, fear, rejection, and disappointment. I choose to return to what You spoke before life interrupted me. Heal my perception where injury distorted my vision, and restore clarity where survival reshaped how I see. By Your Holy Spirit, restore my soul and realign my identity with Your original intention. Where experience has spoken louder than truth, reestablish what You declared first. I choose origin over injury, truth over trauma, and alignment over distortion. I receive restoration without shame and clarity without fear. In Jesus' name, Amen.

Chapter Three
When the Past Tries to Name You

The Voice That Refuses to Stay Silent

The past rarely announces itself as the past. It arrives disguised as logic, caution, and emotional memory. It speaks in familiar tones, using experiences you survived as evidence for why you should limit what you expect next. It does not usually say, "You are no longer who God says you are." Instead, it whispers, "Be careful." "Don't hope too much." "You know how this ends."

Over time, these whispers shape identity. What once happened begins to feel permanent. What was seasonal starts to feel defining. Slowly, subtly, the past attempts to rename the present—not by force, but by repetition.

This is how identity erosion occurs—not through rebellion, but through agreement. A person may still believe, still pray, still desire growth—yet live cautiously because memory has become the loudest voice in the room. And when memory becomes the loudest voice, the future begins to shrink.

Scripture warns us that thought patterns left unchecked can become strongholds rather than testimonies: *"Casting down imaginations, and every high thing that exalteth itself against the knowledge of God." 2 Corinthians 10:5*

The past becomes dangerous when it exalts itself above what God has already spoken. When old experiences are treated as final authority, they begin to compete with truth. The heart stops expecting restoration—not because God has changed, but because the lens of memory has taken over.

This chapter will help you recognize the voice of the past—not to shame you for having memories, but to restore order. Memory was never meant to govern identity. It was meant to inform wisdom while truth remained in authority.

How Memory Transforms into Authority
Memory was never designed to lead. It was designed to remind. Yet when wounds remain unhealed, memory begins to interpret reality rather than simply recall it. A rejection becomes a pattern. A disappointment becomes a prophecy. A delay becomes a verdict.

This is why certain reactions feel automatic. The mind learned to respond before the spirit had time to speak. The heart remembers what it cost to believe, and it tries to protect you from paying that price again. But protection that outlives its season becomes limitation.

The apostle Paul understood this dynamic intimately. His past was not quiet or private; it was violent, public, and deeply opposed to the faith he later carried. Yet Paul refused to allow history to become his authority. *"Forgetting those things which are behind, and reaching forth unto those things which are before."* Philippians 3:13

Paul did not forget in the sense of erasing memory. He forgot in the sense of **withdrawing permission**. His past could testify, but it could no longer govern.

When the Past Speaks Louder Than God's Promise

The past often speaks through emotion rather than reason. It surfaces as hesitation, suspicion of joy, or reluctance to step forward when opportunity presents itself. Many people are not afraid of failure; they are afraid of reliving disappointment. Memory carries feeling, and feeling can feel more convincing than truth when it is left unchallenged. This is how the past gains volume. It does not argue logically—it *feels familiar.* And familiarity, when trusted blindly, becomes persuasive.

This struggle is clearly seen in the journey of Israel after leaving Egypt. Though they were physically free, their thinking remained bound. God had delivered them with power, signs, and clarity, yet their inner world had not yet adjusted to freedom. *"Would to God we had died by the hand of the Lord in the land of Egypt." Exodus 16:3*

This statement reveals the danger of unresolved memory. Egypt no longer held them, but it still named them. Their past became their reference point, even after God proved His presence repeatedly. When hunger arose, memory spoke louder than promise. When discomfort surfaced, fear reinterpreted freedom as risk.

Deliverance happened quickly. Transformation required agreement. God had already spoken freedom, but their memories continued to speak fear. The problem was not that God stopped providing; it was that the people kept measuring the present through the pain of the past. What God intended as a journey toward promise was interpreted as threat because memory had not yet been reordered. This is how promise becomes muted. Not because it is weak—but because it is being evaluated through a lens shaped by survival. When the past speaks louder than God's promise, the future begins to feel unsafe, even when God is present.

Freedom is not only a change of location. It is a change of reference. Until the past is repositioned, promise feels fragile. But when memory is brought back under truth, expectation can grow again. God does not ask people to forget where they have been. He asks them not to let where they have been define where they are going.

This chapter invites that shift. From memory as authority to promise as reference. And when promise becomes the reference point again, movement becomes possible—not because the past disappears, but because it no longer leads.

Joseph: Redefining the Narrative
Joseph's life confronts us with a sobering truth: suffering does not automatically distort identity. It only does so when suffering becomes the primary

interpreter of meaning. Pain has the ability to inform a story, but it was never meant to narrate it.

Joseph experienced betrayal within family, exploitation by authority, and delay without explanation. These were not minor wounds or passing disappointments. They were formative moments—deep enough to justify bitterness, distrust, or resignation. Many people would have allowed these experiences to become defining. Yet Joseph refused to interpret his life solely through pain.

At every stage, Joseph maintained internal alignment even when external circumstances were unstable. His integrity did not collapse under injustice. His sense of purpose did not erode under delay. Even in confinement, Joseph continued to serve, discern, and lead—not because his circumstances were favorable, but because his identity remained anchored.

The clearest evidence of this anchoring appears years later, when Joseph stood face to face with the very people who caused his suffering. In that moment, Joseph had power, position, and justification to retaliate. Instead, he reframed the narrative. *"But as for you, ye thought evil against me; but God meant it unto good." Genesis 50:20*

Joseph did not deny the wrongdoing. He did not minimize the harm. He acknowledged intent clearly—*"ye thought evil."* But he refused to let human intent have the final word. He allowed divine purpose to reinterpret the outcome. This distinction marks maturity.

Healing does not require minimizing pain; it requires allowing God to reassign meaning. Joseph understood that pain explained *what happened*, but purpose explained *why it did not win*. His identity was no longer tethered to betrayal—it was anchored in understanding. Joseph's past did not disappear. It was reordered.

This is what happens when the past is placed beneath truth rather than above it. Memory remains, but it no longer governs identity. Experience is acknowledged, but it does not control expectation. The narrative shifts from *what was done to me* to *what God is doing through me*.

Many people remain trapped, not because they lack forgiveness, but because their story still ends at the wound. Joseph's life shows another way. When God reassigns meaning, the past loses its authority to name the future.

Joseph did not escape suffering. He escaped distortion. And because he did, his life became evidence that identity rooted in truth can outlast even the deepest injury.

Forgiveness: The Moment the Past Loses Its Authority

Forgiveness is often misunderstood as weakness or compliance. Many people associate it with excusing harm, minimizing pain, or surrendering justice. In reality, forgiveness is none of these. Forgiveness is the moment the past loses its power to speak into the future.

Unforgiveness keeps memory alive without redemption. It allows the wound to remain active long after the event has ended. The offense may be over, but its influence continues. When forgiveness is withheld, the past does not remain behind—it becomes a narrator, shaping reactions, expectations, and decisions. This is why unresolved offense feels heavy. It is not just emotional; it is directional. The past continues to interpret the present.

Jesus addressed this directly when He connected forgiveness to freedom rather than morality: *"If ye forgive not men their trespasses, neither will your Father forgive your trespasses."* Matthew 6:15

This statement is often misunderstood as punishment. It is not. It is consequence. What you refuse to release continues to shape you. Forgiveness does not change what happened—but it changes who has authority over what happens next. Forgiveness is not agreement with harm. It is disengagement from its authority.

When forgiveness is withheld, the wound retains influence. It affects how trust is extended, how joy is received, and how risk is approached. The heart remains guarded, not because danger is present, but because memory is still governing perception.

Forgiveness interrupts this cycle. It does not deny pain; it reassigns power. It removes the past from the position of interpreter and returns authority to truth. This is why forgiveness often feels like relief rather than emotion. Something releases—not because the past was justified, but because it was no longer permitted to lead.

Forgiveness is not forgetting. It is deciding what will no longer define you. When forgiveness occurs, the past does not disappear—but it loses its voice. Memory becomes information, not instruction. The wound becomes history, not identity. And the future regains space to form without being filtered through what once hurt.

This is the quiet strength of forgiveness. It does not rewrite the past. It frees the present. And when the past loses its authority, identity can finally move forward—unburdened, clear, and whole.

God's Pattern of Renaming
Throughout Scripture, God does not merely heal people—He renames them. Renaming is not cosmetic; it is covenantal. When God changes a name, He is not correcting behavior; He is redefining identity. The new name does not describe who the person has been—it declares who they are now authorized to become.

A name, in biblical understanding, carries meaning, assignment, and authority. To rename someone is to reposition them. God's pattern of renaming reveals a profound truth: the past may explain a person, but it never outranks God's authority to redefine them. This pattern appears repeatedly.

God renamed **Abram**, whose name meant *exalted father*, to Abraham—*father of many nations*. At the time of this renaming, Abraham had no evidence to support the new identity. His circumstances contradicted the declaration. Yet God did not wait for proof before speaking promise. The new name preceded fulfillment, not the other way around. Renaming was not God's response to Abraham's success; it was God's declaration of Abraham's future.

God also renamed **Jacob**, whose name meant *supplanter* or *deceiver*. Jacob's history was marked by manipulation, fear, and striving. But after an encounter with God, his name was changed to Israel—*one who prevails with God*. God did not deny Jacob's past; He removed its authority. The new name established a new way of relating, living, and leading. Jacob's renaming did not erase his story—it reordered it.

Jesus continued this pattern when He renamed **Simon Peter**. Simon, meaning *listener* or *reed*, was impulsive, inconsistent, and often unstable. Jesus called him Peter—*rock*. This declaration came long before Peter's character aligned with the name. In fact, Peter would later deny Jesus publicly. Yet the name remained.

Jesus did not revoke the name because of failure. The renaming was not conditional—it was authoritative.

These examples reveal something essential: God renames people based on purpose, not performance. Renaming is God's way of removing the past from the position of authority and replacing it with promise. It signals a shift—not just in direction, but in identity. Renaming does not deny history. It ends its governance.

This is why healing alone is not enough. A person may recover emotionally, yet still live under an old name—defined by what happened, what failed, or what was lost. Renaming restores clarity. It gives language to the future. It establishes permission to live forward.

When God renames, He is saying, *You are no longer authorized to live under the old definition.* The past no longer gets to name you. The injury no longer gets to title you. The failure no longer introduces you. God's voice becomes the final reference point. And when identity is renamed by God, the soul begins to align—not by effort, but by agreement. What God speaks begins to govern how a person sees themselves, approaches life, and steps into the future. Renaming is not the end of the journey. It is the beginning of living from truth.

Abram: From History to Promise
Abram's name meant *exalted father*, yet his life openly contradicted the meaning. He was childless, aging, and surrounded by evidence that mocked the very word spoken over him. Every time his name was spoken, it highlighted absence rather than fulfillment. His identity carried tension—between what was declared and what was visible.

Names matter because they are repeated. Abram did not encounter his limitation once; he encountered it daily. Each introduction reinforced the gap between promise and reality. History spoke loudly through repetition. Yet God did not wait for circumstances to change before addressing identity. He did not delay renaming until results appeared. He changed Abram's name while the problem still existed. *"Neither shall thy name any more be called Abram, but thy name shall be Abraham; for a father of many nations have I made thee."* Genesis 17:5

Notice the tense of God's language—*have I made thee*. God spoke from completion, not from process. He did not say *I will make you* after conditions improve. He spoke as though the outcome was already settled. This is how God reclaims authority over identity. He speaks from what He knows, not from what is seen. From that moment forward, Abraham carried promise in his own name. Every time he introduced himself, he spoke agreement with God. Every response required faith. Renaming forced alignment. The mouth could no longer rehearse lack without confronting promise. Renaming required faith because it demanded agreement with God before evidence appeared. Abraham's past infertility no longer had naming rights. History lost its authority to define him. Promise took its place.

God did not rename Abram after Isaac was born—but before. This reveals a critical truth: **identity precedes manifestation**. God changes who you believe you are so that what He promised can follow. Faith is not pretending circumstances do not exist. Faith is choosing which voice has authority. Abraham did not deny his age or his condition. He simply refused to let them outrank what God had spoken.

This is how identity is reclaimed. Not by denying the past—but by removing its authority to name the future. When God renames, He is not asking you to ignore reality. He is asking you to agree with truth *before* reality catches up. And when agreement is established, manifestation is no longer a question of *if*—only *when*.

Jacob: From Survival to Authority

Jacob's name meant *supplanter*, *deceiver*, or *one who grasps*. It described how he lived—securing outcomes through strategy, manipulating circumstances to his advantage, and surviving by control rather than trust. Jacob learned early that blessing felt scarce, so he learned to reach for it. His history shaped his identity, and his identity shaped his behavior. Survival became his language. Striving became his rhythm. Control became his sense of safety.

Jacob's name did not merely describe his past; it governed his present. Every relationship, decision, and movement was filtered through the need to secure what might otherwise be lost. This is how survival identities form—not from malice, but from fear.

Yet when Jacob reached a breaking point—exhausted from striving and afraid of facing his past—God intervened. And He did not intervene with correction alone, but with confrontation and transformation.

Jacob wrestled through the night. This was not merely a physical struggle; it was an internal reckoning. The wrestling exposed the limits of control and the cost of striving. At the end of that struggle, God addressed Jacob not by fixing behavior, but by redefining identity. *"And he said, Thy name shall be called no more Jacob, but Israel: for as a prince hast thou power with God and with men, and hast prevailed."* Genesis 32:28

God renamed Jacob **Israel**, meaning *one who prevails with God*. This new name did not erase Jacob's history; it reframed it. What Jacob once pursued through manipulation, he would now walk in through authority. What he once tried to secure through effort, he would now receive through alignment. The renaming came after wrestling—not after success, and not after perfection. It came after surrender. Jacob stopped striving to control outcomes and allowed God to redefine him.

This reveals a critical principle: **God often renames after surrender, not after perfection**. Transformation does not require flawlessness; it requires agreement. Authority is not born from striving harder—it emerges when striving ends.

Israel walked away with a limp, but he also walked away with clarity. The limp reminded him that strength no longer came from self-reliance. Clarity reminded him that identity no longer came from survival. His past no longer dictated his future. His history no longer named him. God's declaration did.

This is the shift from survival to authority. When the old name is released, the new name governs. And when identity is redefined by God, life no longer has to be grasped—it can be walked in.

Simon: From Instability to Assignment
Simon's name reflected his nature—impulsive, emotional, and inconsistent. His devotion was sincere, but his reactions were often unfiltered. Simon loved deeply, spoke quickly, and acted boldly, yet his confidence frequently outpaced his maturity. His desire was genuine, but his stability was still forming.

Many people recognize themselves in Simon. Passion is present, but consistency feels elusive. Commitment is real, yet fear and pressure expose weakness. Simon was not insincere—he was unfinished.

Jesus did not wait for Simon to stabilize before renaming him. He renamed him while he was still becoming. *"And I say also unto thee, That thou art Peter, and upon this rock I will build my church."* Matthew 16:18

Peter means *rock*—a name that directly contradicted Simon's visible instability. At the moment Jesus spoke it, nothing about Simon's behavior suggested firmness. Yet Jesus spoke identity ahead of evidence. He did not name Simon according to his inconsistency; He named him according to his calling. This is how God speaks. He names people by purpose, not by pattern. He calls out what is being formed, not only what is currently visible. Jesus did not ignore Simon's flaws—but He refused to let them define him.

Even after Peter denied Jesus publicly—at the moment when fear overcame loyalty—Jesus did not revoke the name. He did not strip Peter of assignment. He restored him without renaming him again, because the identity Jesus spoke was never dependent on Peter's performance.

Before the failure ever happened, Jesus had already anticipated restoration: *"And when thou art converted, strengthen thy brethren." Luke 22:32*

Jesus trusted the name He gave more than the failure Peter committed. He spoke beyond the moment. He saw conversion, not collapse. Strength, not shame. Assignment, not disqualification.

This reveals another essential truth: **God's naming is stronger than our weakest moment**. Failure may interrupt expression, but it does not invalidate identity. Inconsistency does not cancel calling—it exposes the need for growth.

Peter's instability did not disqualify him. It revealed where formation was still needed. And once restored, Peter lived into the name he had been given all along. The rock emerged—not because Peter tried harder, but because identity had been settled by Jesus before maturity caught up.

This is the mercy of divine naming. God does not wait for perfection to speak purpose. He speaks purpose so perfection can begin forming.

What Renaming Reveals About God

In each case—**Abraham**, **Israel**, and **Peter**—God renamed before results appeared. He did not wait for behavior to stabilize or for circumstances to confirm identity. He spoke identity first in order to create alignment.

This reveals something essential about God's nature: **He is not reactive**. God does not adjust identity based on performance, nor does He redefine purpose in response to failure. He speaks from intention, not observation. Renaming is not God's response to progress; it is God's declaration of direction. Renaming is God's way of removing the authority of the past and transferring authority to purpose. When God renames, He is not denying what happened—He is ending its jurisdiction. He is saying, *Your history may explain you, but it no longer governs you.*

This is why renaming always precedes movement. A person cannot walk freely into purpose while still answering to an old definition. God addresses identity so the soul can stop negotiating with former names. Scripture summarizes this truth clearly: *"Therefore if any man be in Christ, he is a new creature: old things are passed away; behold, all things are become new."* 2 Corinthians 5:17

This does not mean the past never existed. It means the past no longer holds authority. Old things pass away not because they are forgotten, but because they are no longer permitted to define.

God does not rename to confuse; He renames to clarify. He speaks identity so that the soul can stop answering to survival, shame, fear, or failure. Renaming establishes a new reference point. It tells the heart which voice now carries weight.

What God calls you determines how you move. What He names you establishes what you can carry. And what He speaks over you becomes the standard by which everything else must align. This is why renaming is an act of mercy. God removes the burden of self-definition and replaces it with truth. He does not ask people to figure out who they are—He tells them.

Renaming reveals a God who is committed to purpose over past, clarity over confusion, and truth over trauma. When He speaks a new name, He is not changing His mind about you—He is revealing what He knew all along. And once God's voice becomes the reference point, the past finally loses its authority to speak.

When God Names You, the Past Must Be Silent
The past may remember who you were, but it no longer has permission to address you. Memory may still exist, but authority has shifted. When God speaks a name, He establishes jurisdiction. From that moment forward, the past becomes a reference—not a ruler.

This distinction is critical. A reference informs; a ruler governs. The past can explain context, but it cannot dictate identity. When the soul continues to answer to old names, growth feels slow and effort feels heavy. But when God's voice becomes the reference point, movement becomes lighter and clearer. This is why healing often accelerates when identity is restored. You stop striving to prove worth and begin living from truth. You stop negotiating with insecurity and start responding from alignment. The internal argument quiets—not because the past disappears, but because it no longer has the authority to speak first.

God's pattern of renaming reveals that transformation does not begin with behavior—it begins with agreement. Change becomes sustainable when the heart accepts what God has spoken as final. Agreement is not denial of history; it is a decision about governance.

When you accept what God calls you, you are no longer bound by what life called you. Old labels lose influence. Former definitions fade. The voice that once named you steps aside, not because it was loud, but because it was overruled. This is the moment the past becomes silent—not erased, not ignored, but repositioned. Its role shifts from authority to background. And in that quieting, clarity emerges. You no longer introduce yourself through injury. You no longer interpret life through former names. You no longer wait for permission to live aligned. God has spoken. And what He names, He governs.

When identity is settled this way, the future no longer feels like something to fear. It feels like something to step into—steadily, confidently, without explanation.

Reflective Pause
What Name Have You Been Answering To?
Before you continue, pause for a moment. Consider

the names you have been answering to—some spoken aloud, others repeated silently in your own thoughts. These names may not appear on any document, yet they have shaped how you see yourself, how you approach opportunity, and how you respond under pressure. Ask yourself gently and honestly:

- Which names were assigned by experience rather than by truth?
- Which labels were formed in pain, disappointment, or survival?
- Which identities have you carried because they felt familiar—even if they felt heavy?
- Which descriptions of you have become conclusions, even though they were only seasons?

Now remember what you've seen in Scripture: **God does not allow history to have the final word.** Abram carried the weight of barrenness until God renamed him. Jacob lived from striving until God called him Israel. Simon wrestled with instability until Jesus spoke Peter over him. In each case, the old name described history—but the new name declared purpose.

Reflect on this truth: God does not wait for circumstances to change before He speaks identity. He speaks first, so alignment can follow.

Take a quiet moment and invite the Holy Spirit to show you what He has been calling you—especially in the places where your past has spoken the loudest. Let Him gently expose any name you accepted that no longer agrees with who God created you to be. Do not rush this moment. Restoration often begins in stillness.

When you are ready, continue reading—not as the person your past described, but as the person God is restoring. The past may explain where you have been, but only God has the authority to declare who you are becoming.

Prayer: Releasing Old Names
Father,
I come before You with honesty and openness. I release every name I have accepted that did not originate from You—names shaped by fear, failure, survival, disappointment, or expectation. I lay down every label that no longer agrees with truth. Where my past has spoken loudly, let Your voice become clearer. Where history has tried to define me,

reestablish Your authority. I choose to stop answering to what life called me and begin responding to what You are calling me now. By Your Holy Spirit, quiet every voice that no longer serves purpose. Restore alignment where distortion has lived. Teach my heart to recognize truth and to walk from it without hesitation. I receive the name You speak over me—not earned, not proven, but given. And I move forward from this place with clarity, courage, and peace. In Jesus' name, Amen.

**Chapter Four
Breaking Agreement with False Images**

The Quiet Power of Agreement
Every life is shaped by agreement. Long before actions become habits, and habits become patterns, something is believed. That belief may not always be conscious, but it is powerful. What you agree with internally determines how you move externally.

Agreement is not always deliberate. Often, it forms quietly—through repetition, survival, or unchallenged conclusions. Over time, what was once assumed becomes accepted, and what is accepted begins to govern behavior.

False images do not gain authority because they are true. They gain authority because they are believed.

An agreement is simply a decision—sometimes made unconsciously—to accept something as valid. Once accepted, it begins to shape expectation. Expectation influences choices. Choices reinforce identity. In this way, agreement quietly becomes architecture. This is why many people feel stuck even after healing moments or seasons of clarity. They are not bound by what happened to them; they are bound by what they agreed was true *because* of it. The event may be over, but the agreement remains active.

Agreement also shapes prayer. People often pray from what they believe rather than from what God has spoken. They ask cautiously. They expect little. They protect themselves from disappointment. Not because God is limited—but because agreement has narrowed expectation. Scripture reminds us that agreement carries weight: *"Can two walk together, except they be agreed?" Amos 3:3*

Movement requires agreement. Alignment is impossible where contradiction remains. You cannot move freely into truth while still walking in agreement with distortion. The heart cannot travel in two directions at once.

Breaking agreement is not about self-accusation; it is about clarity. It is the moment when a person recognizes that something they accepted no longer serves truth. Freedom does not begin when circumstances change—it begins when agreement changes.

This chapter will help you identify where false images gained authority—not to shame you for survival, but to restore choice. What was once agreed with can be released. What once governed can be replaced. Truth does not require force. It requires agreement. And when agreement shifts, identity follows.

How False Images Are Formed
False images are rarely formed in moments of rebellion. They are formed in moments of pain, confusion, silence, and survival. They emerge when clarity is absent and the heart must explain what it does not yet understand.

A child interprets absence. A wounded heart explains rejection. A disappointed soul draws conclusions. In these moments, the mind does what it was designed to do—it makes meaning. But meaning formed under pressure is often incomplete. What begins as interpretation slowly becomes belief. Over time, these beliefs harden into internal images—quiet conclusions about who you are and what you can expect:

I am not enough.
I will always struggle.
This is as far as I can go.
God may love me, but He does not trust me.

These images do not shout. They whisper. They shape decisions quietly, influencing what feels safe, what feels possible, and what feels forbidden. They determine how boldly a person speaks, how freely they trust, and how much risk they are willing to take. A person may desire growth, yet hesitate internally because an image has already set a limit.

False images are persuasive because they often feel logical. They are supported by memory, reinforced by experience, and validated by repetition. Over time, they stop feeling like beliefs and start feeling like facts. Scripture describes this process with precision: *"As he thinketh in his heart, so is he."* Proverbs 23:7

What the heart believes, the life follows. Thought becomes posture. Posture becomes pattern. This is why false images must be addressed at the level of agreement, not just behavior. You can change actions temporarily, but if the image remains unchallenged, it will eventually reassert itself. Freedom becomes unstable when belief remains unchanged.

Understanding how false images are formed is not about assigning blame—it is about restoring choice. What was formed in survival can be unformed in truth. What was concluded in pain can be corrected in clarity.

This chapter invites that correction. Not through effort, but through agreement. And when agreement changes, the image begins to change with it.

Gideon: When Fear Shapes Identity
Gideon's story reveals a sobering truth: false images can exist alongside divine calling. A person can be chosen by God and still live beneath his identity. Calling does not automatically correct perception.

When the angel of the Lord appeared to Gideon, he was hiding—threshing wheat in a winepress, away from visibility, driven by fear and scarcity. His location revealed his mindset. He was doing the right thing in the wrong place because survival had become more important than visibility. Fear had not stopped Gideon from working; it had stopped him from standing.

Yet God did not address Gideon according to his posture. He addressed him according to his purpose. *"The Lord is with thee, thou mighty man of valour." Judges 6:12*

This name directly contradicted Gideon's behavior. Gideon was hiding, but God called him mighty. Gideon was afraid, but God spoke courage. Gideon was reducing himself to survive, while God was expanding him to lead. This tension still exists today.

Many people are productive but hidden. They are faithful but afraid. They are capable but cautious. Fear does not always paralyze; sometimes it shrinks visibility. It convinces people to stay small, avoid exposure, decline opportunities, and minimize their voice—not because they lack ability, but because they have learned to associate visibility with risk.

When God spoke to Gideon, Gideon did not argue about God's power. He argued about himself. *"Oh my Lord, wherewith shall I save Israel? behold, my family is poor…and I am the least." Judges 6:15*

Gideon rehearsed limitation fluently. He listed his background, his lack, and his position within his family. His response revealed the image he carried internally. He did not see himself as God saw him; he saw himself through history, comparison, and fear. This is how false images sound today:

I am not qualified enough.

I come from the wrong background.
I do not have the right connections.
I am not as strong, bold, or confident as others.

These statements often feel honest, but they are rooted in agreement with fear rather than alignment with truth. Like Gideon, many people do not struggle with assignment; they struggle with self-perception.

God did not debate Gideon's fear. He did not correct his résumé. He did not elevate his confidence through explanation. Instead, God challenged Gideon's agreement. *"Surely I will be with thee." Judges 6:16*

God shifted the conversation from who Gideon thought he was to who God promised to be. Presence became the antidote to distortion. God's response revealed a principle that still holds true: **identity is stabilized by presence, not performance.**

In today's reality, fear often shapes identity through experiences of rejection, failure, or prolonged waiting. A leader may feel called but hesitate to step forward because a previous attempt ended painfully. A gifted individual may remain silent because their voice was once dismissed. A believer may know God has spoken, yet still question their capacity to carry what was entrusted to them. Like Gideon, they may be hiding—not physically, but emotionally, spiritually, or professionally.

God's answer remains the same. Not reassurance of ability. Not explanation of strategy. But the promise of presence.

When God is present, false images lose authority. Fear no longer defines capacity. Background no longer determines outcome. The image God speaks begins to replace the image fear constructed.

Gideon did not transform overnight. He questioned. He tested. He wrestled. Yet his transformation began the moment he stopped allowing fear to be the final voice and allowed God's presence to become his reference point.

This is the invitation of this passage: not to pretend fear does not exist, but to stop letting it define who you are.

False Images Resist Truth

False images do not disappear simply because truth is presented. They resist. They question. They demand proof. This resistance does not mean a person lacks faith; it means the image has been rehearsed longer than the truth.

Beliefs formed over years do not surrender in a moment. A false image often feels familiar, even when it is harmful. It has been repeated internally, reinforced by experience, and protected by survival. When truth challenges it, the image responds defensively—not because truth is wrong, but because the image fears replacement.

This is why people can hear truth, agree with it intellectually, and still hesitate to live from it. The struggle is not with truth itself, but with the agreement that has governed perception for so long.

Jesus addressed this dynamic directly. He often confronted perception before behavior. *"Why are ye so fearful? how is it that ye have no faith?"* Mark 4:40

Jesus was not condemning fear; He was exposing an agreement. Fear and faith cannot occupy the same agreement space. One will always yield to the other.

The question is not whether truth has been spoken, but which voice has been given authority. False images resist truth by asking questions such as:

What if this doesn't work? What if I'm disappointed again? What if I try and fail?

These questions sound reasonable, but they are rooted in preservation rather than promise. They attempt to keep the heart safe by keeping it small.

Breaking agreement with false images requires more than awareness. Awareness identifies the lie; disengagement removes its power. Disengagement is the intentional decision to stop rehearsing what contradicts what God has spoken—even when the old image feels familiar.

Truth does not force agreement. It invites it. Freedom does not arrive through argument, but through choice. When a person chooses to stop agreeing with fear, truth gains space to govern. And as agreement shifts, resistance weakens. What once felt impossible begins to feel accessible—not because circumstances changed, but because authority did.

This is how false images lose their grip. Not by being silenced externally, but by being released internally.

The Role of the Word in Breaking Agreement
The Word of God functions as a mirror that exposes distortion without condemnation. It does not flatter, and it does not shame. It reveals. Where false images confuse, the Word clarifies. Where experience exaggerates, the Word recalibrates. Scripture describes this discerning power with precision: *"For the word of God is quick, and powerful… and is a discerner of the thoughts and intents of the heart." Hebrews 4:12*

The Word does not merely address behavior; it addresses belief. It penetrates beneath surface reactions and exposes the agreements that shape perception. When the Word enters, it separates truth from assumption, promise from fear, and identity from experience.

This is why reading Scripture often feels confrontational—not because it accuses, but because it interrupts familiar thought patterns. The Word reveals where belief has drifted and where alignment must be restored. It brings into focus what has quietly governed the heart.

Breaking agreement begins when the heart chooses to believe what God says over what experience suggests. This choice is not emotional; it is intentional. It is deciding that truth, not memory, will hold authority. It is allowing Scripture to redefine what feels normal and to challenge what has gone unquestioned.

The Word breaks agreement by repetition. As truth is rehearsed, false images weaken. As God's perspective is returned to daily, old conclusions lose credibility. Over time, the heart begins to respond differently—not because effort increased, but because agreement shifted. This is why sustained transformation requires engagement with the Word. It keeps the mirror clear. It prevents old images from quietly reclaiming influence. And it anchors identity in something unchanging when emotions and circumstances fluctuate.

When the Word governs belief, agreement with distortion cannot remain intact. Truth does not argue with lies—it outlasts them. And as agreement breaks, freedom becomes sustainable.

Replacing Agreement, Not Just Removing It
An agreement cannot simply be removed; it must be replaced. The soul does not live in neutrality. When

one belief is released, another must take its place. What is left empty will eventually be reoccupied. This is why moments of clarity or emotional release, though powerful, are not enough on their own. Without replacement, the mind instinctively returns to what it knows. Familiar patterns re-enter, not because truth failed, but because agreement was left unattended. Jesus explained this principle clearly: *"When the unclean spirit is gone out of a man...he returneth...and taketh with himself seven other spirits." Matthew 12:43–45*

Jesus was not describing a lack of effort; He was revealing the danger of emptiness. Freedom is not sustained by removal alone—it is sustained by replacement. What once governed the heart must be intentionally replaced with what God has spoken.

Breaking agreement with false images means more than rejecting lies; it means actively aligning with truth. This alignment is often challenged by emotion. Feelings may resist. Memories may argue. Old reactions may surface. But agreement is not determined by feeling—it is determined by choice.

Replacement happens when the believer chooses to rehearse God's declarations more consistently than old conclusions. Truth must be spoken, revisited, and returned to—not as a temporary affirmation, but as a governing voice. This is how freedom becomes stable. Not by avoiding lies, but by living filled with truth.

When agreement is replaced, the old image has no place to return. It no longer finds familiarity. It no longer finds authority. The space it once occupied is now governed by truth.

Freedom is preserved when the heart is filled. Identity remains clear when agreement is intentional. And when truth becomes the new agreement, false images lose their ability to reclaim influence.

Guarding New Agreements
New agreements are powerful—but they are also vulnerable. What God establishes in clarity must be protected in practice. Without intentional guarding, even truth can be slowly displaced by familiarity, pressure, or fatigue.

A new agreement does not fail because it was false; it weakens when it is left unattended. Old images often attempt to return quietly, not through dramatic temptation, but through subtle suggestion. They surface in moments of disappointment, comparison, delay, or emotional exhaustion. If left unchallenged, they begin to negotiate again for influence. Scripture instructs us clearly: *"Keep thy heart with all diligence; for out of it are the issues of life." Proverbs 4:23*

Guarding the heart is not about fear—it is about stewardship. What has been restored must be protected. What has been clarified must be preserved. The heart governs direction, and agreement determines what flows from it.

New agreements are guarded through attention. What you consistently listen to, rehearse, and allow to shape your thinking reinforces what you believe. Truth remains strong when it is revisited regularly. Silence, when left unmanaged, often becomes an invitation for old conclusions to speak again.

Guarding agreement also requires discernment. Not every voice deserves influence. Not every memory deserves rehearsal. Not every thought deserves agreement. The discipline of discernment is learning when to pause, question, and realign before a thought settles into belief.

Scripture reminds us of this responsibility: *"Take heed what ye hear" (Mark 4:24).* What you allow in determines what takes root.

Guarding new agreements does not mean perfection. It means responsiveness. When you notice drift, you return. When old images attempt to reassert themselves, you choose alignment again. Each return strengthens clarity and weakens distortion. This is how transformation becomes durable. Not through intensity, but through consistency. Not through effort, but through attention.

New agreements are preserved by repetition, protected by discernment, and strengthened through continued alignment with truth. When guarded well, they no longer feel new—they become normal. And when truth becomes normal, false images lose their influence quietly and completely.

Choosing Alignment Over Familiarity
False images often feel familiar because they have been lived with for a long time. They have explained disappointments, justified caution, and provided emotional shelter during difficult seasons. Over time, these images become familiar companions—known, predictable, and seemingly safe.

Truth, however, often feels unfamiliar at first. It challenges what has been rehearsed. It confronts internal narratives that once served survival but no longer serve purpose. This is why healing can feel unsettling, even when it is right. The heart has learned how to function within distortion, and clarity requires relearning.

Familiarity should never be mistaken for accuracy. Something can feel normal and still be untrue. A belief can feel protective and still be limiting. Many people remain bound, not because truth is unavailable, but because distortion feels safer than change.

This tension appears clearly in daily life. A person may stay in environments that diminish them because those environments feel known. A gifted individual may silence her voice because visibility once brought criticism. A believer may continue living beneath his calling because stepping forward feels uncertain. These are not signs of weakness; they are signs of learned familiarity.

Healing, therefore, requires a deliberate choice. It is the choice to align with truth even when it feels uncomfortable. Alignment often precedes emotional relief. The mind must agree with truth before the heart feels safe enough to follow. Scripture describes this process clearly: *"And be not conformed to this world: but be ye transformed by the renewing of your mind." Romans 12:2*

Transformation does not begin with external change. It begins with internal agreement. The renewal of the mind is the slow, intentional replacement of familiar distortions with God's truth. This renewal reshapes how decisions are made, how identity is understood, and how purpose is pursued.

Choosing alignment over familiarity is not rejection of your past; it is refusal to be governed by it. It is the moment you stop allowing old narratives to define what is possible. It is the decision to believe God's Word above emotional memory, even when memory feels convincing. Transformation begins when agreement shifts—when truth becomes the new reference point and familiarity loses its authority.

Reflective Pause
What Are You Still Agreeing With?
Before you continue, pause for a moment and consider what agreements may still be shaping your decisions. Not the ones you openly reject—but the

ones that quietly influence what you expect, what you avoid, and what you believe is possible. Ask yourself with honesty and compassion:
- What thoughts surface most quickly when something does not go as planned?
- What explanations do you automatically give for limitation, delay, or hesitation?
- What beliefs feel familiar—even if they no longer feel true?
- Where might you still be choosing comfort over alignment?

Notice where your reactions are shaped more by past experience than by present truth. These reactions are not failures; they are signals. They reveal agreements that may need to be released or replaced.

Take a moment to identify one belief you have accepted simply because it felt safe or familiar. Do not argue with it. Just acknowledge it. Awareness is often the first step toward change.

Now consider this truth: alignment begins when you choose to believe what is true, not just what feels comfortable. You are not required to have everything resolved before you move forward. You are only asked to remain open and willing to realign.

Do not rush this pause. Growth often begins quietly, when old agreements are gently recognized and new ones are allowed to take their place.

When you are ready, continue reading with a renewed awareness—not as someone trying to change themselves, but as someone learning to live from truth.

Prayer: Releasing and Replacing Agreements
Father,
I come before You with openness and honesty. I acknowledge the agreements I have carried—some formed in pain, some in fear, some in survival. Where I accepted conclusions that no longer reflect truth, I choose to release them now. I ask You to replace every false image with what You have spoken. Where familiarity has guided my decisions, realign me with truth. Where comfort has limited my growth, establish clarity. Teach my heart to agree with what is right, even when it feels unfamiliar. By Your Holy Spirit, guard the new agreements You are forming within me. Keep my mind attentive, my heart responsive, and my identity anchored in truth. Help me to recognize when old beliefs attempt to return and to choose alignment again without hesitation or

shame. I receive freedom that is sustained, clarity that is steady, and identity that is rooted. I choose to live from truth—not temporarily, but consistently. In Jesus' name, Amen.

Chapter Five
The Word of God as the True Mirror

Why Every Other Mirror Eventually Fails

Every human being lives by a mirror. The question is not whether you are looking into one, but which one you are trusting. Identity is always shaped by reflection. Something is always speaking back to you—interpreting your worth, your capacity, and your place in the world.

Some look into the mirror of emotion. Others into achievement, approval, comparison, or past experience. Each of these mirrors reflects something real, but none of them were designed to define identity. They offer feedback, not truth. Emotions fluctuate. Success fades. Approval changes. Memory distorts.

When any of these become the primary mirror, identity becomes unstable. Confidence rises and falls with performance. Worth is negotiated through response. Direction becomes reactive instead of anchored. A person may appear strong externally while remaining uncertain internally, because the mirror they are using cannot sustain clarity.

God never intended feelings, people, or circumstances to be the source of self-understanding. He intended His Word to be the mirror that remains constant when everything else shifts. Unlike other mirrors, the Word does not reflect mood, outcome, or opinion. It reflects truth. Jesus affirmed this clearly: *"Sanctify them through thy truth: thy word is truth." John 17:17*

Truth is not what feels strongest in a moment. Truth is what God has spoken and continues to stand by. It does not change with seasons. It does not adjust to pressure. It does not contradict itself to accommodate experience. This is why every other mirror eventually fails. They were never meant to carry the weight of identity. They respond to conditions; the Word establishes condition. They describe circumstances; the Word defines essence.

When the Word becomes the mirror, identity no longer needs constant reinforcement. Clarity becomes steady. Confidence becomes quiet. Purpose becomes anchored. The soul stops searching for validation because it has found reflection in something unchanging.

This chapter invites you to shift mirrors—not to dismiss emotion, experience, or achievement, but to reposition them. They can inform you, but they must not define you. Only the Word was designed to tell you who you are without distortion. When the Word becomes the mirror, identity stops fluctuating and begins to stabilize. And stability changes everything.

The Word Reveals Without Wounding
Human mirrors often exaggerate flaws or hide strengths. They highlight what is convenient and obscure what is inconvenient. Some magnify weakness until it feels permanent; others inflate strength until it becomes fragile. The Word of God does neither. It reveals with accuracy and love. It does not distort, shame, or flatter. It simply tells the truth.

This is what makes the Word a safe mirror. It does not injure the soul in order to correct it. It reveals what is present without attaching condemnation. It exposes distortion without humiliation and corrects error without accusation. James gives language to this divine function: *"For if any be a hearer of the word, and not a doer, he is like unto a man beholding his natural face in a glass."* James 1:23

The Word shows what is actually there—not what fear assumes or pride projects. It reflects reality without agenda. When a person looks into the Word, they are not being evaluated by performance or compared to others. They are being invited into clarity.

This is why the Word is restorative rather than harsh. It does not confront to punish; it reveals to align. Where human mirrors wound through judgment or silence, the Word heals through truth. It does not deny weakness, but it does not define a person by it, either.

Many believers read Scripture for comfort, instruction, or inspiration—but not for reflection. Reflection requires vulnerability. It allows the Word to speak into internal narratives that have gone unchallenged for years. It invites the reader to see not only what they are doing, but what they have been believing.

When the Word becomes the mirror, confusion begins to lift. False conclusions lose credibility. Old self-definitions are gently corrected. Clarity replaces uncertainty—not through force, but through truth received.

The Word does not wound the heart to reshape it. It reveals the heart so that alignment can occur. And when clarity replaces distortion, healing follows naturally.

Why Circumstances Make a Poor Mirror
Circumstances are persuasive but unreliable. They speak with urgency, yet they lack authority. A season of loss may suggest abandonment. A season of waiting may suggest disqualification. A season of weakness may suggest inadequacy. These conclusions often feel logical because they are reinforced by emotion and repetition.

Yet circumstances are interpreters, not authors. They describe what is happening, but they do not define what is true. When allowed to function as a mirror, they distort identity by tying worth to outcome and meaning to timing. Scripture contradicts this instability with clarity: *"God is not a man, that he should lie." Numbers 23:19*

Situations describe conditions, but Scripture declares truth. Circumstances change quickly; truth does not. When circumstances become the mirror, identity rises and falls with results. Confidence strengthens during success and weakens during delay. Hope fluctuates with momentum. The soul becomes reactive rather than anchored.

When the Word becomes the mirror, identity remains steady regardless of season. Waiting no longer threatens worth. Delay no longer suggests failure. Difficulty no longer implies abandonment. The Word reminds the believer that truth is not determined by what is visible, but by what has been spoken. This distinction matters deeply in today's world, where comparison, pressure, and performance constantly demand self-evaluation. Without a stable mirror, people live exhausted—continually recalculating worth based on external feedback. They adjust expectations repeatedly, protect themselves unnecessarily, and measure progress by outcomes rather than alignment.

The Word interrupts this cycle. It offers a reference point that does not shift with circumstance. It allows the believer to stand steady when life is unstable and to remain confident when evidence feels contradictory. Circumstances may report the season, but the Word reveals the identity. And when identity is anchored in truth, seasons lose their power to redefine the soul.

David: Recalibrating the Soul with the Word

David's life reveals the discipline of returning to truth when emotions overwhelm perception. He did not deny his feelings, suppress them, or spiritualize them away. He interrogated them. David understood that emotions are real, but they are not reliable guides for identity. *"Why art thou cast down, O my soul? and why art thou disquieted within me?"* Psalm 42:5

This question reveals awareness rather than avoidance. David noticed his inner state, but he did not surrender authority to it. He refused to let emotion narrate meaning or determine direction. Instead, he brought emotion into conversation with truth. After questioning his soul, David gave it instruction: *"Hope thou in God."*

This is not denial—it is recalibration. David acknowledged the presence of distress, then realigned his inner world with truth. He did not wait for his feelings to change before responding rightly. He chose alignment first, trusting that emotion would follow clarity. This practice is essential for emotional maturity. Mature faith does not ignore emotion; it governs it. Feelings inform, but they do not lead. They signal internal conditions, but they must not define identity. The Word provides the standard by which emotions are interpreted rather than obeyed. David returned to the Word repeatedly because he understood its stabilizing power. When fear rose, he rehearsed truth. When discouragement surfaced, he anchored himself in God's promises. When confusion threatened clarity, he recalibrated his soul through Scripture.

This discipline is still necessary today. Many people allow emotion to become their primary mirror. A bad day becomes a bad identity. A season of heaviness becomes a conclusion about worth or direction. David shows a different way. He teaches us that the soul must be trained to listen to truth more than it listens to feeling. The Word recalibrates what emotion exaggerates. It steadies what pressure destabilizes. It anchors what uncertainty shakes. When the Word becomes the mirror, emotions no longer dominate perception. They find their proper place—acknowledged, but not obeyed. And when truth governs the inner world, the soul regains balance.

Jesus: Living From the Word as Identity
Jesus Christ Himself modeled this reality with clarity and restraint. In the wilderness—hungry, isolated,

and physically vulnerable—He did not negotiate with emotion or interpret His condition as meaning. He did not reason with appetite, pressure, or expectation. He anchored Himself in Scripture. *"It is written, Man shall not live by bread alone, but by every word that proceedeth out of the mouth of God." Matthew 4:4*

This moment reveals more than resistance to temptation. It reveals how identity is sustained. Jesus did not quote Scripture to prove strength; He quoted Scripture to affirm source. He was not responding to hunger alone—He was establishing what truly governs life. Jesus lived from the Word, not from circumstance. Hunger did not define Him. Isolation did not destabilize Him. Pressure did not redirect Him. The Word served as His reference point, grounding Him in truth when conditions suggested lack. This reveals a profound principle: **the Word does not merely guide behavior; it stabilizes identity**. When identity is rooted in Scripture, external pressures lose their leverage. Temptation does not gain power because there is nothing unsettled to exploit.

Each temptation in the wilderness attempted to question identity before it questioned action. *If thou be the Son of God...* Yet Jesus never defended His identity emotionally. He reinforced it scripturally. He did not argue. He did not explain. He returned to what had already been spoken. This is how the Word functions as a mirror. It reflects truth consistently, regardless of circumstance. It reminds the soul who it is when the environment attempts to suggest otherwise.

When the Word becomes the mirror, temptation loses its advantage—not because temptation disappears, but because identity is already secure. The heart is not searching for validation, relief, or confirmation. It is anchored. Jesus demonstrates that clarity is maintained not by willpower, but by reference. Not by effort, but by agreement. Not by resisting pressure, but by living from truth. And when identity is anchored this way, life no longer responds to circumstance—it responds from truth.

How the Word Corrects Inner Narratives
The Word of God carries authority to contradict internal dialogue that feels deeply personal. Many inner narratives sound convincing because they have been repeated privately for years. They feel personal, familiar, and even logical. Yet familiarity does not equal truth.

The Word does not argue with these narratives emotionally; it exposes them structurally. It separates what was assumed from what was spoken. It distinguishes between interpretation and truth. Scripture describes this discerning function clearly: *"For the word of God is quick, and powerful...and is a discerner of the thoughts and intents of the heart."* Hebrews 4:12

This means the Word reaches beneath surface thoughts and identifies the agreements beneath them. It reveals not only what you are thinking, but *why* you are thinking it. In doing so, it brings clarity where confusion once felt normal.

Correction, in this sense, is not rejection. It is protection. When the Word corrects the mirror, it prevents the heart from settling into conclusions that quietly limit growth, confidence, and direction. It interrupts beliefs that feel self-protective but ultimately confining.

Over time, believers who reflect consistently in the Word begin to notice a shift. They pause before agreeing with negative self-talk. They question fear-driven assumptions. They resist shame-based reactions that once felt automatic. The Word becomes a filter—screening thoughts before they become beliefs. This practice does not silence emotion; it reorders authority. Feelings are acknowledged, but they are no longer trusted blindly. Thoughts are noticed, but they are no longer accepted without examination. Truth becomes the standard by which everything else is evaluated.

As this alignment deepens, inner dialogue begins to change naturally. Old narratives lose credibility. New ones take root—not because effort increased, but because truth gained influence. When the Word governs the inner world, the mirror remains clear. And clarity protects destiny quietly, consistently, and without force.

Living Daily from the True Mirror
When the Word of God becomes the mirror, transformation becomes sustainable rather than seasonal. Identity no longer requires constant repair because it is anchored in something that does not shift with emotions, circumstances, or human opinion. A life rooted in Scripture is not immune to difficulty, but it is insulated against distortion.

Many believers experience moments of clarity in worship, prayer, or after reading an encouraging book, yet struggle to maintain that clarity in daily life. This does not reflect a lack of sincerity. More often, it reveals a lack of consistent reflection. Healing that is not reinforced by truth must be repeatedly recovered.

The Word of God was never intended to be visited occasionally. It was designed to be lived with daily. *"Thy word is a lamp unto my feet, and a light unto my path." Psalm 119:105*

Notice the language of Scripture. A lamp does not illuminate an entire lifetime at once; it provides light for the next step. This is how the Word functions practically. It does not overwhelm the believer with everything at once. It guides moment by moment, decision by decision, thought by thought.

Reading the Bible daily is not merely a religious discipline; it is daily recalibration. Each time Scripture is opened, truth is given the first voice before emotion, memory, pressure, or opinion attempts to shape perception. The Word resets the internal compass. Without this recalibration, believers often live reactively. They respond to stress, conflict, disappointment, or pressure based on instinct or past experience. The Word interrupts this pattern by creating a pause between stimulus and response. It teaches the believer how to respond from truth rather than react from injury. This is how believers begin to live healed rather than triggered. When the Word is familiar, triggers lose their authority because truth is already present. Confidence grows—not because circumstances improve, but because identity is settled. Groundedness replaces defensiveness because the soul no longer feels the need to prove or protect itself. Practically, living from the true mirror means allowing Scripture to speak into ordinary moments. It means returning to the Word when a thought arises that contradicts peace. It means measuring decisions against what God has said rather than how fear interprets the situation. It means pausing to ask, *What does the Word say about this?* before agreeing with discouragement, comparison, or self-doubt.

This practice does not require long hours or perfect routines. It requires intention and consistency. Even a small portion of Scripture, read attentively and reflected on honestly, can realign an entire day. Over time, the Word reshapes thinking patterns, emotional responses, and expectations. Scripture describes this process as renewal: *"And be renewed in the spirit of your mind." Ephesians 4:23*

Renewal is ongoing. It occurs as the Word becomes familiar enough to surface naturally when pressure arises. A believer who lives daily from the true mirror begins to recognize when thoughts are misaligned, when emotions exaggerate reality, and when fear attempts to speak louder than faith.

The mirror of the Word does not change, even when seasons do. God's truth remains steady in times of abundance and in times of lack, in clarity and in confusion, in joy and in grief. When life feels fragmented, the Word provides continuity. It holds the soul together when circumstances pull in different directions.

To live daily from the true mirror is to allow Scripture to become the place you return to—not only for answers, but for identity. It is where you remember who you are before the world tells you who to be. This is not about perfection. It is about posture. A heart that consistently turns toward the Word will gradually begin to reflect the truth it beholds.

Reflective Pause
Which Mirror Are You Using?
Before you move on, pause for a moment and consider what has been shaping your self-

understanding most consistently. Not what you *intend* to look to—but what you actually return to when pressure rises, when disappointment appears, or when uncertainty sets in. Ask yourself quietly:

- When I feel unsettled, what do I look to for reassurance?
- What voices most often interpret my experiences—emotion, memory, opinion, or truth?
- Where do I seek clarity first: circumstance or Scripture?
- What has been shaping my inner dialogue more than I realized?

Notice without judgment which mirror you have been using. This pause is not about correction; it is about awareness. What reflects you most often will influence you most deeply.

Now consider this: the Word of God offers a reflection that does not shift with mood, outcome, or season. It does not exaggerate weakness or inflate strength. It simply reveals truth.

Take a quiet moment and imagine returning to that mirror—not occasionally, but consistently. Allow the idea of daily reflection to feel possible rather than demanding. Transformation rarely happens in dramatic moments; it often unfolds through faithful, repeated alignment.

When you are ready, continue reading with this awareness: clarity is not something you chase. It is something you return to. And the mirror you choose will determine what you see.

Prayer: Living from the True Mirror
Father,
I choose to return to truth as my reference point. I acknowledge the mirrors I have trusted—emotion, circumstance, memory, or approval—and I release their authority to define me. I realign my heart with Your Word, which remains steady when everything else shifts. Teach me to return to Scripture not only for answers, but for identity. When pressure rises or confusion attempts to speak, help me pause and listen for truth. Recalibrate my thoughts, steady my emotions, and anchor my decisions in what You have spoken. By Your Holy Spirit, make the Word familiar within me. Let it rise naturally when fear tries to lead, when doubt attempts to interpret, and when old narratives resurface. Establish clarity that endures and confidence that is quiet and secure. I choose to

live from the true mirror—daily, consistently, and without striving. In Jesus' name, Amen.

Chapter Six
When Comparison Distorts the Mirror

The Subtle Theft of Identity

Comparison rarely announces itself as danger. It enters quietly—disguised as motivation, curiosity, or self-evaluation. It begins with observation and slowly becomes measurement. What started as awareness turns into judgment—first of others, then of self. Comparison does not ask, *What has God given me?* It asks, *Why does theirs look different?*

This shift is subtle, but significant. The mirror moves away from truth and toward contrast. Identity is no longer formed by calling, but by comparison. Instead of seeing yourself through God's intention, you begin seeing yourself through someone else's outcome, timing, or visibility.

The danger of comparison is not admiration; it is distortion. Admiration can inspire. Comparison competes. It quietly reframes worth, making progress feel inadequate and uniqueness feel like deficiency. It turns difference into disqualification.

Comparison also fragments focus. Attention moves outward, away from purpose and into evaluation. The soul becomes preoccupied with measuring instead of aligning. Joy diminishes. Confidence weakens. Direction blurs—not because God has changed His plan, but because the mirror has shifted. Scripture warns against this subtle trap with clarity: *"But they measuring themselves by themselves, and comparing themselves among themselves, are not wise." 2 Corinthians 10:12*

Comparison is not wisdom; it is misalignment. It replaces truth with relative standards and assigns value based on proximity rather than purpose. It teaches the heart to look sideways instead of upward. When comparison governs perception, identity becomes unstable. A person may feel confident one moment and diminished the next, depending on who they are observing. Worth fluctuates. Peace erodes. The mirror no longer reflects truth—it reflects contrast.

This chapter invites a return to alignment. Not by isolating yourself from others, but by restoring the correct reference point. Identity was never meant to be formed by comparison. It was meant to be received. When the mirror is recalibrated, comparison loses its power. And when truth regains authority, identity stabilizes again.

Why Comparison Feels So Convincing

Comparison feels convincing because it appeals to visibility. You can see what others are doing, accomplishing, or receiving, but you cannot see the full context of their journey. You see outcomes without understanding process. You see fruit without knowing roots. Visibility creates an illusion of completeness, when in reality you are only seeing fragments.

This is what makes comparison persuasive. It presents partial information as full truth. It invites conclusions without context. And when conclusions are drawn without understanding, identity begins to drift.

In today's world, comparison is intensified by constant exposure. Social media, professional environments, ministry platforms, and even family gatherings provide endless opportunities to measure progress. Lives are curated. Success is highlighted. Struggle is often hidden. Without discernment, comparison slowly reshapes how a person evaluates themselves.

A person may begin to question their calling because someone else's path appears faster. A believer may feel inadequate because another's gift appears more visible or celebrated. A leader may shrink because someone else's success feels louder or more affirmed. None of these reactions indicate a lack of faith. They indicate misplaced focus.

Comparison convinces because it bypasses purpose and fixates on timing. It ignores assignment and emphasizes outcome. It shifts attention away from what God is forming and toward what others are displaying. In doing so, it quietly reframes value. The danger is not noticing difference; it is interpreting difference as deficiency. When comparison becomes the lens, uniqueness feels like delay, and process feels like failure. What is still unfolding begins to feel behind.

Comparison also creates impatience. It pressures the soul to rush what God is still shaping. It tempts the heart to abandon faithfulness in pursuit of visibility. Over time, it erodes contentment and replaces it with quiet dissatisfaction. This is why comparison must be confronted at the level of perception. The issue is not what you see—it is how you interpret what you see. When focus is restored to purpose rather than proximity, comparison loses its influence.

Clarity returns when the mirror is corrected. And when identity is anchored in truth, visibility no longer determines worth.

Saul and David: When Comparison Turns Destructive

Scripture presents **Saul** as a man who began well. He was chosen by God, anointed for leadership, and entrusted with authority over Israel. His calling was legitimate, and his assignment was clear. Yet Saul's downfall did not begin with rebellion; it began with comparison.

Comparison quietly introduced insecurity into Saul's leadership. As long as Saul focused on God's instruction, he led with confidence. However, the moment **David** emerged and received public favor, Saul's internal stability began to erode. *"And Saul eyed David from that day and forward." 1 Samuel 18:9*

This verse reveals more than jealousy. It reveals insecurity. Saul did not suddenly lose his anointing, nor was his position threatened in that moment. What changed was his perception of himself. He stopped seeing himself through God's calling and began evaluating his worth through David's success.

Insecurity always shifts focus outward. It replaces purpose with suspicion and assignment with anxiety. Saul moved from leading to watching, from obedience to comparison, and from confidence to self-preservation. This pattern remains painfully relevant today.

Leaders become threatened by those they were meant to mentor. Believers question their value because someone else is advancing. Gifted individuals diminish themselves because attention has shifted. Insecurity rarely announces itself as fear; it often disguises itself as caution, discernment, or concern.

Saul did not lose his assignment because David succeeded. He lost clarity because comparison repositioned his focus. Instead of stewarding what God had given him, Saul became preoccupied with protecting his position.

Comparison did not merely trouble Saul; it consumed him. He measured his worth against applause, attention, and affirmation rather than obedience. His peace became dependent on how others responded to David rather than on how he responded to God. In contrast, David's stability reveals a different posture. David did not build his identity through reaction or recognition. Even when pursued unjustly, he refused to define himself by Saul's insecurity. *"The Lord is my light and my salvation; whom shall I fear?" Psalm 27:1*

David's confidence was not rooted in comparison; it was anchored in identity. He trusted God's timing rather than chasing validation. He honored Saul even when Saul dishonored himself, because David understood that identity secured by God does not need to compete. Insecurity always seeks control. Identity seeks alignment.

Saul's insecurity led him to grasp, accuse, and isolate. David's identity led him to wait, trust, and remain faithful. Saul's fear distorted his leadership; David's faith preserved his future. This contrast reveals a sobering truth: comparison does not only distort how we see others—it distorts how we see ourselves. When identity is not anchored in God, the success of others feels threatening rather than inspiring.

The tragedy of Saul's story is not that David rose. It is that Saul allowed insecurity to redefine him. He forfeited peace not because God withdrew favor, but because he stopped trusting the favor he had already been given.

Comparison distracted Saul. Identity anchored David. And the same choice confronts every heart today.

Comparison Weakens Gratitude and Distorts Timing

Comparison not only distorts identity; it distorts perception of timing. It convinces people they are late when they are actually in process. It suggests delay when God is cultivating depth. What is still forming begins to feel behind simply because someone else appears further along.

Comparison erodes gratitude quietly. Instead of recognizing what God is developing in the present season, attention shifts to what has not yet manifested. The heart becomes impatient with process and dismissive of preparation. Growth that requires time begins to feel like absence rather than intention.

This tension is evident in Scripture when **Peter**, freshly restored by **Jesus Christ**, turned his focus away from his own calling and toward another disciple. *"Lord, and what shall this man do?"* John 21:21

Peter was not asking out of curiosity alone. He was measuring his future against someone else's. In that moment, comparison threatened to interrupt obedience. Jesus responded firmly and clearly: *"What is that to thee? follow thou me." John 21:22*

This response reveals a critical truth: comparison distracts from obedience. Jesus did not explain **John**'s assignment, nor did He justify Peter's. He redirected focus. Purpose cannot be pursued sideways. Clarity is lost when attention shifts away from what God has spoken personally.

Comparison tempts the heart to evaluate timing through proximity rather than obedience. It encourages questions like: *Why is theirs unfolding faster?* or, *Why does mine look different?* These questions feel reasonable, but they subtly undermine trust. They assume that God works on a single timeline rather than through individual processes.

When comparison governs perception, gratitude weakens. Faithfulness begins to feel unnoticed. Preparation feels unnecessary. Yet Scripture consistently affirms that God works intentionally within seasons.

Delay does not mean denial. Process does not mean punishment. Timing does not indicate favor or failure.

Comparison causes people to rush what God is refining and to resent what God is shaping slowly. But when focus returns to obedience, peace is restored. Gratitude resurfaces. The heart learns to honor its own season without diminishing another's. Jesus' instruction remains relevant: *Follow me.*

When obedience becomes the focus, timing no longer feels threatening. The believer learns to trust that what God is doing now is preparing them for what comes next. Comparison fades, and gratitude regains its place. Clarity is restored when the mirror is corrected. And when gratitude returns, trust deepens.

The Illusion of Equal Timelines
God does not measure progress by speed. He measures it by alignment. Two people may be called, gifted, and faithful, yet their journeys unfold differently. Timing is not uniform because purpose is not generic.

Comparison assumes identical timelines, but Scripture reveals divine specificity: *"To every thing there*

is a season, and a time to every purpose under the heaven."
Ecclesiastes 3:1

This verse does not describe randomness; it reveals intention. Seasons are assigned. Timing is purposeful. God works within distinct rhythms, shaping each life according to what it is meant to carry.

When you compare your season to someone else's harvest, discouragement often follows. You may begin to question your faithfulness, your obedience, or your calling—when in reality, you are simply in a different phase of formation. What you are building may require depth before visibility, pruning before expansion, or silence before influence.

Comparison ignores this necessary preparation. It demands premature conclusions. It pressures the heart to evaluate progress through exposure rather than through obedience. As a result, what is still being formed begins to feel delayed or deficient.

Scripture consistently shows that visibility is not the measure of readiness. Many whom God prepared privately were revealed publicly only after their inner life could sustain the weight of influence. Timing protected purpose, not hindered it.

The illusion of equal timelines creates unnecessary strain. It tempts people to rush what God is refining and to despise seasons meant for strengthening. But when alignment becomes the measure instead of speed, peace returns.

You are not behind. You are not late. You are not overlooked. You are in a season that serves purpose—even if it does not resemble someone else's. When identity is anchored in God, timing no longer feels threatening. It feels intentional. Comparison fades when trust deepens. And when trust deepens, patience becomes possible.

Returning the Mirror to God
The remedy for comparison is not isolation; it is realignment. Withdrawing from others does not heal distortion—restoring the mirror does. Identity must be returned to God, where worth is measured by calling rather than competition, and purpose is affirmed without contrast.

When the mirror reflects God's truth, comparison loses its grip. Gratitude replaces envy. Confidence replaces insecurity. Peace replaces pressure. The heart no longer scans for validation because it has returned to its source. Scripture describes this posture with clarity: *"Let every man prove his own work, and then shall he have rejoicing in himself alone, and not in another." Galatians 6:4*

This is not a call to self-focus; it is a call to alignment. Rejoicing in your own work does not mean dismissing others—it means recognizing the value of what God has entrusted to you. It is understanding that your assignment does not compete with another's, and your season does not diminish someone else's progress.

Returning the mirror to God restores perspective. Instead of measuring progress by proximity to others, the believer begins to measure faithfulness by obedience. Instead of asking *How do I compare?* the heart begins to ask *Am I aligned?*

This shift brings freedom. The soul is released from the exhausting cycle of comparison and allowed to rest in purpose. Identity stabilizes because it is no longer being evaluated against changing standards. When God becomes the mirror, identity finds rest. When alignment replaces comparison, clarity returns.

And when clarity governs perception, the soul can move forward without pressure.

This is the quiet strength of a heart anchored in God: it celebrates others without shrinking, advances without competing, and lives fully from the identity God has already affirmed.

Living Free from the Comparison Trap
Living free from comparison is a discipline, not a destination. It is not achieved once and forgotten; it is practiced daily through intentional alignment. Freedom is sustained by remembrance—remembering who you are, whose you are, and what God has uniquely entrusted to you.

Comparison often returns quietly. It surfaces in moments of fatigue, waiting, or transition. This is why freedom requires returning to the Word when comparison whispers lies about worth, timing, or progress. Truth must be revisited regularly so that distortion does not regain influence.

Practically, living free from comparison means learning to celebrate others without diminishing yourself. It means honoring another person's growth without interpreting it as a commentary on your own.

It means resisting the urge to measure obedience against outcome or faithfulness against visibility. It also means trusting that God is equally intentional with every life, even when paths differ. Different timing does not imply unequal favor. Different processes do not suggest unequal purpose. God's work is personal, precise, and purposeful. Scripture reassures us of this truth: *"The steps of a good man are ordered by the Lord." Psalm 37:23*

Your steps are ordered—not rushed, not delayed, not overlooked. What feels slow may be strategic. What feels quiet may be preparatory. God orders steps according to destination, not comparison.

When this truth is embraced, comparison loses its grip. Peace replaces pressure. Gratitude replaces insecurity. Confidence becomes quiet and grounded rather than reactive. The soul no longer needs to compete—it learns to trust.

Living free from comparison allows identity to settle. The heart becomes steady, the mind becomes clear, and the spirit becomes secure. Life is no longer lived sideways, scanning for reference, but forward—anchored in purpose.

This is the freedom of alignment: to walk your path fully, to honor others sincerely, and to trust God completely. And when comparison no longer defines perception, identity remains whole.

Reflective Pause
Where Has Comparison Been Speaking?
Before you continue, pause for a moment and consider where comparison may have been influencing your thoughts, emotions, or expectations—often quietly, without notice.
Ask yourself gently and honestly:
- Where have I been measuring my progress against someone else's visibility or outcome?
- When have I interpreted delay as failure or silence as neglect?
- Whose journey have I been using as a reference point instead of God's voice?
- Where might comparison have weakened my gratitude or unsettled my peace?

Notice these areas without judgment. Awareness is not condemnation; it is clarity. Comparison often operates unnoticed, shaping perception before it is recognized.

Now consider this truth: your path was designed with intention. Your timing is purposeful. Your process is not accidental. What God is forming in you cannot be rushed or replicated.

Take a quiet moment and return the mirror to God. Release the need to measure yourself through contrast. Allow gratitude to rise for what He is doing in your life now, even if it looks different from others. When you are ready, continue reading with renewed focus—not as someone behind or overlooked, but as someone being led deliberately. Comparison loses power when alignment is restored.

Prayer: Releasing Comparison
Father,
I release every agreement with comparison. Where I have measured myself against others instead of Your Word, realign my vision. Teach me to celebrate without envy and to trust Your timing without pressure or fear. Restore my focus to the path You have set before me. Establish my identity in what You have spoken, not in what others display. Quiet every voice that distracts from obedience, and anchor my heart in gratitude for the season You are shaping. I choose alignment over comparison, trust over

pressure, and faithfulness over visibility. In Jesus' name, Amen.

When the mirror returns to God, comparison loses its authority, and the soul finds freedom through divine alignment.

Chapter Seven
The Role of Faith: Seeing Beyond What Is

Faith Begins Where Sight Ends

Faith does not deny reality, but it refuses to be ruled by it. It acknowledges what is visible without allowing the visible to become final. Faith begins where sight ends—not because sight is wrong, but because sight is limited. What is seen explains conditions; faith discerns direction.

Many believers misunderstand faith as optimism or positive thinking. Biblical faith is neither denial nor imagination. It is spiritual perception—the ability to see through God's Word what has not yet manifested in the natural. Faith does not ignore facts; it places facts under truth. Scripture defines faith with clarity: *"Now faith is the substance of things hoped for, the evidence of things not seen." Hebrews 11:1*

Faith gives substance to hope and evidence to what has not yet appeared. It allows the believer to live with confidence even when circumstances have not yet aligned with promise. Faith supplies assurance before confirmation and steadiness before results. This is why faith becomes essential when identity is being restored. Without faith, the heart waits for evidence before agreeing with truth. With faith, the heart agrees with God first and allows evidence to follow. Faith makes room for alignment before visibility.

Faith does not replace wisdom, nor does it dismiss process. It simply refuses to let delay rewrite identity or uncertainty redefine calling. Where sight asks, *What is happening?* faith asks, *What has God spoken?*

Living by faith means learning to interpret life through promise rather than through pressure. It means trusting God's Word even when feelings fluctuate, progress feels slow, or outcomes remain unseen. Faith anchors identity in truth while the external world is still catching up.

This chapter explores how faith sustains clarity during delay, strengthens identity under pressure, and enables the believer to move forward without needing immediate proof. Faith is not passive waiting—it is active trust. And when faith governs perception, the mirror remains clear—even when circumstances are still forming.

Seeing Through God's Perspective

To live by faith is to see life from God's perspective rather than from current conditions. This does not mean ignoring difficulty or minimizing reality; it means interpreting difficulty through truth. Faith does not change what is happening—it changes how what is happening is understood. Paul captured this posture with clarity: *"For we walk by faith, not by sight." 2 Corinthians 5:7*

Walking by faith is not passive. It is an intentional decision to allow God's Word to define meaning, direction, and expectation. Sight reports what is visible. Faith discerns what God is doing within and beyond what is seen. Sight describes the present; faith interprets it through promise.

This distinction becomes crucial in seasons of waiting, uncertainty, or contradiction. When circumstances do not yet reflect what God has spoken, sight alone will always conclude prematurely. It will interpret delay as absence, resistance as denial, and silence as neglect. Faith interrupts those conclusions by anchoring perception in God's character rather than in current conditions.

Seeing through God's perspective requires trust. It requires believing that God is at work even when progress is not immediately measurable. Faith allows the believer to remain steady when outcomes are still forming and to continue moving forward without needing constant confirmation.

Without faith, the heart grows weary and the mind becomes restless—searching for reassurance in circumstances that cannot provide it. With faith, endurance is strengthened because hope is anchored. The believer learns to wait without anxiety, to trust without striving, and to move without fear. Faith reframes the question. Instead of asking, *Why is this happening?* Faith asks, *What is God forming through this?*

When life is seen through God's perspective, confusion gives way to clarity. The believer no longer reacts to what is unfolding but responds from what has been spoken. Faith becomes the lens that keeps identity intact while circumstances are still catching up. And when perception is governed by faith, the mirror remains aligned—even when the view ahead is not yet clear.

Abraham: Trusting Beyond Evidence

Abraham's journey illustrates the true essence of faith because it unfolds in direct contradiction to visible evidence. God spoke promise into a life that, by every measurable standard, suggested limitation rather than possibility. Abraham was advanced in age, his body no longer responsive to youthful strength, and his wife Sarah was barren. Time, biology, and social expectation all testified against the word God had spoken. Faith, in Abraham's case, was not built on optimism. It was forged in tension.

Every day Abraham woke up surrounded by reminders that contradicted the promise. His body testified to weakness. His household reflected absence rather than inheritance. His age suggested endings rather than beginnings. Yet God's promise remained unchanged, steady, and uncompromising. Scripture captures Abraham's response with deliberate clarity: *"Who against hope believed in hope, that he might become the father of many nations." Romans 4:18*

This verse does not suggest denial of reality. It reveals discernment. Abraham did not pretend the evidence did not exist; he refused to let evidence define truth. Faith did not require him to ignore his condition—it required him to **reorder authority**. Hope according to circumstance had expired. Hope according to God had just begun.

Abraham's faith was not passive agreement; it was active trust. He continued to walk, obey, and respond to God even while the promise remained unfulfilled. Every step forward was an act of alignment with a future he could not yet see. Scripture emphasizes this inner posture: *"He staggered not at the promise of God through unbelief; but was strong in faith, giving glory to God." Romans 4:20*

Strength in faith did not mean absence of questions. It meant refusal to withdraw trust. Abraham learned to praise before proof, to honor God before outcome, and to live as though God's word carried greater weight than physical limitation.

This is the cost of faith. It asks the believer to agree with God before confirmation appears. It demands obedience without guarantees, trust without timelines, and perseverance without immediate reward. Faith requires living from what God has said rather than from what circumstances suggest.

In today's reality, this tension is deeply familiar. Many believers carry promises that appear delayed by time, restricted by resources, or contradicted by experience. Faith invites them into the same posture Abraham embraced—not denial of facts, but **submission of facts to truth.** Faith does not change evidence instantly. It changes **alignment immediately.**

Abraham's story reminds us that God is not intimidated by limitation. He is not delayed by age, hindered by history, or restricted by probability. When God speaks, He speaks from completion, not from process. *"Is any thing too hard for the Lord?" Genesis 18:14* Faith answers this question not with explanation, but with agreement.

To trust beyond evidence is to place God's Word above every visible contradiction. It is to live in obedience while waiting, to remain confident while evidence argues otherwise, and to keep walking even when the destination feels distant.

Abraham did not become the father of many nations by seeing first. He became it by **believing first.** And this remains the invitation of faith today.

Faith Sustains Identity During Delay
Faith plays a critical role in sustaining identity during seasons of delay. Delay is not merely a pause in

movement; it is a testing ground for perception. Without faith, delay is often interpreted as rejection, abandonment, or failure. With faith, delay is understood as preparation, alignment, and refinement.

The danger of delay is not time itself, but **misinterpretation**. Many people lose confidence not because God has withdrawn, but because waiting has distorted how they see themselves. When answers do not come quickly, the heart is tempted to conclude that something is wrong—not just with circumstances, but with identity.

Faith corrects this distortion by anchoring expectation in **God's character**, not in calendars or outcomes. It reminds the believer that silence does not equal absence, and waiting does not equal denial. Scripture assures us with unwavering clarity: *"Being confident of this very thing, that he which hath begun a good work in you will perform it." Philippians 1:6*

This verse is not a motivational statement; it is a declaration of divine commitment. Faith rests in the assurance that God does not abandon what He initiates. What He begins, He sustains—even when progress feels invisible.

Joseph's life illustrates this truth vividly. He received a dream that clearly spoke of leadership and elevation, yet years passed before any visible fulfillment appeared. Betrayal, false accusation, and imprisonment marked his journey, but delay did not redefine his identity. Scripture consistently records that **the Lord was with Joseph**, even when Joseph's circumstances suggested otherwise.

Joseph did not spend his years of waiting trying to manufacture fulfillment. He remained faithful where he was, allowing character to mature before position arrived. Faith preserved his identity so that delay did not turn into bitterness or self-doubt.

David's story reveals a similar pattern. Anointed as king while still a shepherd, David lived through years of obscurity, danger, and pursuit. The oil was real, but the throne was distant. Faith sustained David's identity during this gap. He did not force the promise, retaliate against Saul, or compromise his integrity to accelerate the process. David understood that timing belongs to God, not to impatience.

This is where many believers struggle today. In a culture that values speed, visibility, and immediate results, delay feels like failure. People attempt to self-correct prematurely—changing direction, lowering expectations, or abandoning what God spoke because waiting feels uncomfortable. Faith resists this impulse. Faith refuses to redefine calling based on discomfort. It holds identity steady when emotions fluctuate and circumstances remain unresolved. Faith says, *"God is still working, even when I cannot see evidence yet."*

This does not mean passivity. It means **steadfastness**. Faith remains obedient without rushing. It stays aligned without forcing outcomes. It trusts that preparation is happening even when progress feels slow.

Jesus Himself modeled this posture. Though fully aware of His mission, He spent thirty years in obscurity before beginning public ministry. Delay did not confuse His identity because His confidence was rooted in the Father, not in public affirmation.

Faith teaches the believer to wait without shrinking, to trust without withdrawing, and to remain whole without immediate validation. Delay tests patience. Faith preserves identity.

What God has begun in you is not fragile. It does not depend on perfect timing, constant confirmation, or uninterrupted progress. Faith trusts that what God starts, He finishes—and that no season of waiting has the authority to redefine who you are.

Peter: Learning to See Beyond the Storm
Peter's experience on the water offers a powerful illustration of faith's relationship with perception. When Jesus called Peter out of the boat, Peter walked on water—not because the storm ceased, but because his focus was fixed. *"But when he saw the wind boisterous, he was afraid; and beginning to sink." Matthew 14:30*

The moment Peter shifted from faith-based vision to circumstance-based sight, fear entered. The storm did not change; Peter's focus did.

This story reveals a critical truth: **faith is sustained by focus.** When attention remains anchored in Christ, fear loses leverage. When attention shifts to conditions, instability follows.

Faith Is Built Through the Word
Faith is not self-generated; it is cultivated. It does not rise from effort alone, nor does it sustain itself through emotion or willpower. Scripture makes it

clear that faith has a source, and that source is truth consistently received. *"So then faith cometh by hearing, and hearing by the word of God."* Romans 10:17

Faith grows through repeated exposure to what God has spoken. The more the Word shapes perception, the more naturally faith rises. When Scripture becomes familiar, trust becomes instinctive. Faith is strengthened when God's promises are rehearsed more frequently than life's contradictions. This is why the Word must be heard, not merely known. Hearing implies reception, attention, and openness. It means allowing Scripture to enter beyond the intellect and settle into belief. Over time, the Word trains the heart to recognize truth even when circumstances attempt to argue otherwise. Scripture affirms this strengthening process: *"Thy word have I hid in mine heart, that I might not sin against thee."* Psalm 119:11

When the Word is internalized, it becomes a safeguard. It steadies the believer during pressure and anchors decision-making when clarity feels distant. Faith grows because truth is already present within. The Word also sustains hope during waiting and uncertainty: *"For whatsoever things were written aforetime were written for our learning, that we through patience and comfort of the scriptures might have hope." Romans 15:4*

Scripture does not merely inform; it comforts and reinforces hope. It reminds the believer that God's dealings are consistent and His character dependable. In practical terms, this is why daily engagement with Scripture matters. The Word trains the believer to see beyond the immediate and to trust beyond the visible. When truth is encountered regularly, faith becomes resilient rather than reactive, steady rather than seasonal. Faith built through the Word does not collapse under pressure because it is rooted in something eternal.

Faith Produces Movement, Not Passivity

Biblical faith always leads to action. It does not rush ahead of God, but it does not remain stagnant either. Faith moves in obedience even when clarity feels partial. James emphasizes this reality: *"Faith, if it hath not works, is dead." James 2:17*

Faith responds to God's Word with obedience. It steps forward even when the path is not fully visible, trusting that light will appear with movement. This is how faith transforms identity into action. What the heart believes, the life eventually follows.

Living by Faith Daily
Living by faith does not require dramatic gestures or constant spiritual intensity. It is practiced quietly through daily trust, consistent obedience, and steady confidence that is rooted in God rather than in circumstances. Faith is exercised in ordinary decisions—choosing truth when fear offers alternatives, choosing obedience when shortcuts seem appealing, and choosing trust when outcomes remain uncertain.

Daily faith is revealed in posture more than performance. It is the decision to believe God's character when situations feel unresolved and to remain aligned with His Word when emotions fluctuate. Faith does not eliminate questions, but it keeps those questions from controlling direction.

Faith allows the believer to remain steady when life feels unstable. It creates inner assurance even when external confirmation is delayed. This steadiness is not the absence of challenge; it is the presence of trust. When faith governs daily life, pressure does not easily dislodge peace, and uncertainty does not immediately erode confidence.

Scripture captures this way of living with simplicity and authority: *"For the just shall live by faith."* Habakkuk 2:4

This statement does not describe an occasional experience; it defines a lifestyle. Faith is not reserved for crisis moments or major decisions alone. It is the framework through which the believer interprets daily life, responds to challenges, and navigates uncertainty. To live by faith daily is to consistently choose alignment over anxiety and truth over fear. It is not about having all the answers, but about trusting the One who does. Faith becomes the atmosphere in which the believer lives—not a reaction to difficulty, but a way of walking forward with quiet assurance. Faith, then, is not a moment. It is a way of living.

Prayer: Strengthening Spiritual Sight
Father,
I ask You to strengthen my faith. Where my vision has been limited by what I see, teach me to see through Your Word. Help me to trust You beyond evidence and to walk in obedience even when clarity feels incomplete. Anchor my heart in truth, and let faith guide my steps daily. In Jesus' name, Amen.

When faith becomes your way of seeing, fear loses its grip, and the future becomes a place of trust rather than uncertainty.

Chapter Eight
God's Plan vs. Man's Plans

Life Is Always Being Directed by a Plan

Every life moves according to a plan—whether that plan is intentional or assumed. No one drifts accidentally. Direction is always influenced by something: beliefs, expectations, voices, or pressures that quietly shape decisions over time. Even choosing not to plan is, in itself, a form of planning.

What many people do not realize is that **multiple planners can influence a single life at the same time.** Some plans are loud and obvious, openly directing choices and priorities. Others are subtle and persistent, operating beneath awareness through habits, fears, and learned patterns. Without discernment, a person can unknowingly live under plans that were never meant to define them. Scripture acknowledges this reality with clarity: *"There are many devices in a man's heart; nevertheless the counsel of the Lord, that shall stand." Proverbs 19:2*

Human intentions may be many, layered, and sincere, but they are not final. God's plan does not compete for authority—it **outlasts** it. It stands firm even while other plans attempt to assert influence, redirect focus, or quietly take control. This truth establishes a foundation for everything that follows: Life is not shaped by the loudest plan, but by the one given authority.

Personal Plans: Desire, Fear, and Control
Personal plans often begin with sincerity. They are formed from desire, ambition, fear of loss, or a longing for stability. People plan to protect themselves from disappointment, to manage uncertainty, or to create a sense of control in an unpredictable world. In many cases, these plans are not born from rebellion but from responsibility and survival.

There is wisdom in planning. Scripture affirms foresight, diligence, and stewardship. Yet danger arises when personal plans become rigid—when they are held tightly rather than surrendered freely. When plans are formed without submission, they can quietly replace trust. What begins as responsibility can evolve into control, and what begins as vision can turn into pressure.

At this point, planning no longer serves peace; it produces anxiety. The heart becomes preoccupied with outcomes rather than obedience, and success becomes something to manage rather than something to trust God with. Scripture offers balance and clarity: *"Commit thy works unto the Lord, and thy thoughts shall be established." Proverbs 16:3*

God does not ask believers to abandon planning; He asks them to submit it. Plans surrendered to God remain flexible, teachable, and responsive. They allow room for redirection without resistance. Plans driven by fear, however, resist correction. They cling tightly to certainty and become sources of tension rather than peace.

When personal plans are aligned with God, they serve purpose. When they are driven by control, they quietly compete with trust. Alignment is revealed not by whether a person plans, but by how willing they are to release those plans when God speaks differently.

Family and Generational Plans
Families often plan with sincere and loving intentions. They desire stability, continuity, and success for those they care about. These plans are usually formed from protection rather than control, shaped by what previous generations learned through hardship, sacrifice, and survival.

Yet family expectations can become powerful forces, shaping decisions long before a person recognizes their influence. Generational plans often define what success should look like, which paths feel acceptable, and which dreams appear too risky or unrealistic. These expectations can provide guidance—but they can also quietly limit calling when tradition outweighs discernment.

Some people feel internal conflict, not because they lack direction, but because they are torn between honoring where they come from and obeying where God is leading them. This tension is not rebellion; it is discernment awakening. Jesus acknowledged this tension clearly, without dishonor or rejection: *"For I came down from heaven, not to do mine own will, but the will of him that sent me." John 6:38*

Jesus did not dismiss family, tradition, or community. He simply established priority. Obedience to God sometimes requires the courage to walk paths others did not plan for you—even when those plans were made in love.

God's plan does not reject family, but it is not confined by generational expectation. It honors heritage without being restricted by it. When God's direction differs from what has been assumed or inherited, alignment requires trust—not defiance, but clarity. A life fully aligned with God's plan learns to honor family while following God, respect history without being ruled by it, and appreciate legacy without allowing it to replace calling.

Community and Cultural Influence
Communities shape values, pace, and perception. Culture quietly plans what is celebrated, rewarded, or ignored. It sets standards for success, timelines for achievement, and unspoken definitions of worth. Over time, these influences begin to feel normal—rarely questioned, often assumed.

Community provides belonging, and culture offers structure, but both can also create pressure to conform. Cultural plans often emphasize visibility, speed, and comparison. They reward quick results, public affirmation, and measurable outcomes. God's plan, however, prioritizes formation, depth, and obedience. What culture applauds quickly, God often builds patiently. Scripture speaks directly to this tension: *"Be not conformed to this world: but be ye transformed by the renewing of your mind." Romans 12:2*

Conformity happens quietly. It does not require conscious rebellion—only repeated exposure without discernment. Over time, cultural expectations can begin to shape identity, convincing people to measure progress by applause, productivity, or visibility rather than by faithfulness and alignment.

God's plan often feels countercultural because it resists urgency and refuses shallow metrics. It values character over image, obedience over popularity, and long-term fruit over immediate recognition. While culture pressures people to move faster, God often calls them to move deeper.

Alignment with God requires intentional resistance to cultural pressure—not withdrawal from community, but discernment within it. It is learning to belong without being governed, to participate without surrendering conviction, and to live faithfully even when God's pace differs from what is socially rewarded.

When culture defines success, the soul becomes restless. When God defines direction, the soul becomes steady.

Friends and Familiar Voices

Friends influence direction through counsel, observation, and shared experience. Their voices often carry weight because they know history, personality, and context. Familiar voices feel safe, trusted, and reasonable—especially during moments of uncertainty or transition.

Yet even well-meaning counsel can unintentionally redirect purpose when advice is rooted in fear, limited perspective, or personal bias. What sounds protective may actually be restrictive. What sounds practical may quietly contradict what God has spoken. Scripture reminds us where true wisdom originates: *"Counsel is mine, and sound wisdom." Proverbs 8:14*

God's wisdom does not dismiss human counsel, but it discerns it. Alignment matters more than agreement. Not every voice that cares for you is equipped to direct you. Advice can be sincere and still be misaligned with God's timing, method, or intention. This is why discernment is essential. God often confirms direction through peace, Scripture, and the witness of the Holy Spirit rather than through consensus. Familiar voices may urge caution when God is inviting courage, or recommend safety when God is calling for faith.

Following God sometimes means listening carefully—then choosing obedience over comfort. It requires valuing relationships without allowing them to replace revelation. When God's voice is clear, familiarity must yield to truth.

True alignment is not proven by how many agree with you, but by how faithfully you respond to what God has spoken.

The Enemy's Plan: Distraction and Distortion
The enemy's plans rarely announce themselves through chaos alone. More often, they operate through distraction, delay, compromise, or discouragement. Rather than attacking destiny directly, the enemy targets identity—because when identity is distorted, direction soon follows. Scripture speaks to this reality with sober clarity: *"Be sober, be vigilant; because your adversary the devil, as a roaring lion, walketh about, seeking whom he may devour." 1 Peter 5:8*

This warning is not an invitation to fear; it is a call to awareness. Vigilance protects focus. Discernment guards direction. A distracted believer may remain active while slowly drifting from alignment.

The enemy's strategy often involves subtle redirection. An opportunity may appear productive yet quietly pull the heart away from obedience. A delay may feel harmless but gradually erode confidence. A compromise may seem small but weaken spiritual clarity over time. Discouragement, left unaddressed, can slowly persuade a person to settle beneath what God has spoken. This is why discernment matters. Not every open door is divine, and not every resistance is opposition. Some doors distract; some obstacles refine. Wisdom lies in recognizing the difference.

God's plan leads toward clarity, peace, and alignment—even when the path is challenging. The enemy's plan leads toward confusion, pressure, and fragmentation—even when the path looks reasonable. One strengthens identity; the other slowly erodes it.

Remaining aligned requires attentiveness. It is choosing truth over urgency, obedience over convenience, and purpose over distraction. When identity is anchored in God, distortion loses influence, and distraction loses its power to redirect.

God's Plan: Eternal, Redemptive, and Precise
God's plan stands above every competing influence because it is formed from eternal wisdom rather than limited information. While human plans are shaped by perspective, urgency, and partial understanding, God's plan is shaped by complete vision. He sees the past, present, and future simultaneously, without fragmentation or guesswork. Scripture captures this distinction clearly: *"For my thoughts are not your thoughts, neither are your ways my ways, saith the Lord." Isaiah 55:8*

God's plan accounts for what people often overlook—character, timing, long-term impact, and generational legacy. Where others plan for convenience, God plans for transformation. Where humans plan for immediate relief, God plans for lasting fruit. His purposes are not rushed by pressure, nor weakened by delay.

One of the most comforting truths about God's plan is its redemptive nature. Nothing is wasted—not even missteps, interruptions, or seasons that felt confusing at the time. *"And we know that all things work together for good to them that love God." Romans 8:28*

This does not mean all things are good. It means God is skilled at redeeming what others misuse, restoring what was delayed, and realigning what was disrupted. Detours do not disqualify destiny when the plan belongs to God. Even what felt like interruption becomes instruction under His care.

God's plan is precise, not fragile. It does not collapse under pressure, nor does it unravel because of human limitation. When a life is surrendered to God's counsel, alignment brings peace—not because the path is easy, but because it is ordered.

The difference between every other plan and God's plan is this: Other plans attempt to manage life. God's plan transforms it. When His plan is trusted, identity stabilizes, direction clarifies, and the soul rests—not in certainty of outcome, but in confidence of guidance.

Yielding Without Losing Hope
Yielding to God's plan does not mean surrendering desire; it means trusting God to shape desire correctly. Faith learns to release control without releasing vision. It allows God to refine purpose without diminishing promise.

Many people fear yielding because they associate it with loss. In God's economy, yielding is not subtraction—it is alignment. What is surrendered is not erased; it is ordered. God does not remove hope when He redirects a plan. He preserves it by anchoring it in wisdom rather than urgency. This kind of yielding produces peace—not because every outcome is clear, but because direction is secure. The heart rests, not in certainty of timing, but in confidence of guidance. Scripture anchors this posture: *"Trust in the Lord with all thine heart; and lean not unto thine own understanding." Proverbs 3:5*

Trust requires releasing the need to fully understand before obeying. It is choosing God's counsel over personal calculation. As yielding deepens, anxiety loosens its grip—not because challenges disappear, but because alignment strengthens confidence.

Clarity often follows obedience. Peace grows as the soul learns that God's plan is not fragile, delayed, or threatened by surrender. When God's plan becomes the reference point, hope remains intact—and the heart moves forward without fear.

Reflective Pause
Whose Plan Is Guiding Your Direction?
Before continuing, take a quiet moment to consider the plans currently shaping your life. Not the plans

you speak about publicly, but the ones influencing your decisions internally. Ask yourself honestly:
- Which plans have been guiding my recent choices—God's, mine, or someone else's?
- Where have I been holding tightly out of fear rather than trust?
- What have I been trying to control that God may be inviting me to surrender?

Consider that yielding to God does not erase desire; it realigns it. Releasing control does not diminish purpose; it clarifies it. What feels uncertain in your hands may be secure in God's. Allow the Holy Spirit to gently reveal any plan you have been living under that no longer aligns with God's counsel. Do not rush this moment. Alignment often begins with awareness.

When you are ready, continue—not with pressure to understand everything, but with willingness to trust the One who sees fully. Your direction does not depend on perfect planning. It depends on surrendered alignment.

Prayer: Surrendering Competing Plans
Father,
I bring before You every plan that has influenced my

life—plans formed by desire, fear, family expectation, cultural pressure, and opposition. I release control and choose alignment with You. Where my plans are misaligned, gently correct me. Where I have rushed ahead of You, teach me patience. Where I have hesitated in fear, strengthen my trust. I choose Your counsel above every other voice. I trust that Your plan is good, intentional, and complete—even when I cannot yet see the full picture. Shape my direction according to Your wisdom, and establish my steps in truth. In Jesus' name, Amen.

When God's plan becomes your foundation, every other plan finds its proper place—or loses its authority.

Chapter Nine
From Reflection to Revelation

When Seeing Turns Into Knowing

Reflection allows you to see yourself clearly, but revelation allows you to understand **why** you see what you see. Reflection shows the image; revelation explains the meaning behind it. Without revelation, reflection can remain passive—informative but unresolved. With revelation, clarity begins to shape direction.

Many people reach a place where they recognize patterns, wounds, strengths, and distortions. They can name what happened and how it affected them, yet still feel uncertain about what comes next. Reflection answers the question, *"What do I see?"* Revelation answers the question, *"What is God saying about what I see?"* Scripture describes this shift clearly: *"The entrance of thy words giveth light; it giveth understanding unto the simple." Psalm 119:130*

Light reveals. Understanding mobilizes.

Moses' encounter at the burning bush illustrates this transition with remarkable clarity. Moses noticed a bush that burned without being consumed. At first, he was simply observing something unusual. He saw, but he did not yet understand. *"And Moses said, I will now turn aside, and see this great sight." Exodus 3:3*

This moment represents reflection. Moses was attentive. He was curious. He recognized that something was happening, yet observation alone did not change his direction. It was not until God spoke that sight turned into knowing.

When God addressed Moses from the bush, revelation entered the moment. God did not merely explain the fire; He explained Moses. God revealed who He was, what He was doing, and why Moses was standing there. What Moses had seen externally now carried internal meaning. *"I have surely seen the affliction of my people…and I am come down to deliver them." Exodus 3:7–8*

In that moment, Moses' reflection became revelation. The burning bush was no longer just a phenomenon; it was a summons. What Moses had been observing became a call to participate. This is the nature of revelation. It takes what you have noticed about yourself, your life, and your history, and places it within God's purpose. Moses had long reflected on his failure in Egypt, his inadequacy, and his obscurity in Midian. Revelation reframed all of it—not as disqualification, but as preparation. Seeing alone would have left Moses standing still. Revelation mobilized him.

Why Reflection Alone Can Leave You Stuck
Reflection without revelation can quietly become a cycle. A person may gain awareness yet remain motionless. They understand their pain, their failure, and their limitations, but they do not understand **what God is doing with it**. They see the pattern, but not the path forward. This is why some people remain emotionally aware yet spiritually hesitant. They can articulate what shaped them, but they cannot discern what God is forming through it. Reflection names the wound; revelation assigns meaning.

The life of **Moses** illustrates this tension clearly. After Moses killed the Egyptian, he fled Egypt in fear. Scripture tells us that Moses ran not only from Pharaoh, but from the consequences of his own actions. In Midian, Moses lived for forty years with reflection but without revelation. He was aware of his failure, his rejection, and his displacement. He knew what he had done wrong, and he adjusted his life accordingly.

Moses reflected deeply—perhaps too deeply. He had once believed he could deliver his people. Now he believed he was disqualified. His reflection produced withdrawal rather than movement. He built a quiet life, far from Egypt, far from conflict, and far from calling. Reflection without revelation convinced Moses that obscurity was safer than obedience. This is the danger of reflection alone. It explains *why* you ran, but it does not tell you *where to go next*. It helps you survive, but it does not help you fulfill purpose.

Moses' forty years in Midian were not wasted, but they were incomplete. Reflection had shaped humility, but without revelation it had also reinforced limitation. Moses had interpreted his past failure as final rather than formative. Revelation was what interrupted this cycle.

When God spoke from the burning bush, He did not deny Moses' past. He redefined it. What Moses had seen as failure, God revealed as preparation. What Moses had interpreted as rejection, God reframed as positioning. Revelation took Moses' history and placed it within divine intention. This is what revelation does. It reframes experience through heaven's perspective. It does not erase pain; it redeems it. It does not minimize failure; it repurposes it. Revelation introduces divine meaning where reflection alone had only produced self-assessment. Without revelation, Moses would have remained a shepherd in Midian—aware, reflective, and stuck. Revelation turned awareness into assignment. This is why reflection, though necessary, is not sufficient. Healing awareness must be followed by divine understanding. Otherwise, insight becomes introspection without movement. Revelation does not rush the soul, but it **releases it**.

Peter: When Revelation Redefines Identity
Peter's journey demonstrates how revelation shifts identity, not just understanding. Peter had spent time with Jesus, observed miracles, and listened to teaching. Yet proximity alone had not yet produced clarity. When Jesus asked, *"Whom say ye that I am?"* Peter responded from revelation, not observation. *"Thou art the Christ, the Son of the living God."* Matthew 16:16

Jesus immediately clarified the source of Peter's insight: *"Flesh and blood hath not revealed it unto thee, but my Father which is in heaven."* Matthew 16:17

This revelation changed Peter's position. Jesus did not simply affirm Peter's answer; He redefined Peter's identity and authority. Revelation elevated Peter from follower to foundational voice. This reveals an essential truth: **revelation does not just inform—it authorizes**. When God reveals truth, He often follows it with responsibility. Identity shifts because understanding deepens.

The Holy Spirit: Interpreter of Meaning
Revelation does not come from effort alone. It is not produced by intense thinking, emotional processing, or repeated analysis of the past. Revelation is **imparted**. It is given. And the One who imparts it is the Holy Spirit. The Holy Spirit does more than remind us of Scripture or recall moments from our history. He **interprets meaning**. He takes what we have lived through and reveals what God has been doing within it. He connects experience to purpose and pain to preparation in a way human reasoning cannot accomplish on its own. Scripture affirms this role clearly: *"But God hath revealed them unto us by his Spirit." 1 Corinthians 2:10*

This means that true understanding is not self-discovered; it is Spirit-revealed. A person may revisit the same memory for years and remain confused until the Holy Spirit illuminates it. When He does, what once felt fragmented suddenly aligns.

The Holy Spirit reveals progressively. He does not overwhelm the heart by exposing everything at once. He knows the capacity of the soul and the timing of healing. What He reveals, He does so with care, wisdom, and precision. This is why understanding often comes in stages. A season that once felt meaningless begins to make sense years later. A delay that once felt like loss is later recognized as protection. A disappointment that once felt devastating is eventually seen as redirection. The past itself does not change, but **perspective matures**. Jesus spoke of this process when He said: *"I have yet many things to say unto you, but ye cannot bear them now."* John 16:12

The Holy Spirit reveals what is necessary for the current season. He does not reveal truth to burden, but to free. He explains not to accuse, but to heal. He brings clarity that stabilizes rather than overwhelms. This is why revelation often feels gentle rather than dramatic. It settles the heart. It quiets inner conflict. It brings peace even before answers are complete. The Spirit reassures the believer that

God has been present all along, even in moments that felt confusing or silent.

When the Holy Spirit interprets meaning, the believer stops asking only, *"Why did this happen to me?"* and begins to ask, *"What is God forming through this?"* This shift changes everything. Pain no longer defines identity. Experience no longer feels wasted. The heart begins to trust that nothing surrendered to God is without purpose. What once felt confusing begins to feel purposeful—not because the journey was easy, but because understanding has matured. The Holy Spirit has a way of revealing God's hand in places where the mind only saw loss.

This is the sacred work of the Spirit: to turn reflection into revelation, confusion into clarity, and history into testimony.

The Emmaus Road: When Revelation Reignites Direction

The journey of the Emmaus disciples illustrates how revelation transforms confusion into movement. After the crucifixion, these disciples were walking away from Jerusalem—away from purpose—while discussing disappointment and unanswered questions.

They were reflecting, but they were not yet understanding. Jesus walked with them, yet they did not recognize Him. It was not until revelation came that direction changed. *"And their eyes were opened, and they knew him." Luke 24:31*

The moment revelation occurred, confusion lifted. Their reflection turned into recognition. And immediately, their direction reversed. *"And they rose up the same hour, and returned to Jerusalem." Luke 24:33*

Revelation did not merely comfort them; it **repositioned them**. What they once walked away from, they now ran back toward. This demonstrates that revelation restores clarity, urgency, and assignment.

Revelation Brings Peace Before Details
One of the marks of true revelation is peace without full explanation. God rarely reveals the entire picture. He reveals enough to require trust.

Abraham moved with revelation, not with full information. *"By faith Abraham…went out, not knowing whither he went." Hebrews 11:8*

Revelation tells you *where* to step without always explaining *how the journey will unfold.* Faith fills the space between instruction and outcome.

From Revelation to Obedience

Revelation is never an end in itself. It is an invitation. What God reveals is meant to be responded to, not merely admired or analyzed. This is why revelation must be protected by obedience. Truth that is received but not acted upon gradually loses its clarity. It does not disappear instantly; it fades quietly, becoming something once known but no longer lived. Scripture emphasizes this connection between understanding and response with unmistakable clarity: *"Be ye doers of the word, and not hearers only, deceiving your own selves." James 1:22*

This warning is not harsh; it is protective. It reminds us that spiritual insight without action can create a false sense of growth. A person may feel enlightened, comforted, or inspired, yet remain unchanged if revelation is not translated into obedience. Obedience is the bridge between knowing and becoming. When revelation is obeyed, confidence grows—not because everything suddenly becomes easy, but because trust is reinforced through movement. Each step taken in response to truth strengthens assurance that God is guiding the path. Fear diminishes, not because uncertainty vanishes, but because obedience confirms alignment.

Direction often becomes clearer *after* movement begins. God rarely reveals the entire path at once. He reveals enough to invite trust, then clarifies further as obedience continues. This is why many believers experience greater clarity while moving than while standing still.

Obedience also protects the heart from stagnation. Revelation that is delayed indefinitely can turn into hesitation, and hesitation can quietly become resistance. Obedience interrupts this drift by keeping the soul responsive and open.

It is important to understand that obedience does not require perfection. It requires willingness. God does not ask for flawless execution, but for faithful response. Even small acts of obedience—changing a habit, releasing a burden, making a decision, taking a step—honor the revelation God has given.

Throughout Scripture, those who responded quickly to revelation grew in clarity and authority. Those who delayed often struggled with confusion. This is not because God withdrew, but because movement sharpens discernment.

When revelation is obeyed, it becomes anchored in experience. Truth moves from concept to conviction, from inspiration to transformation. The heart begins to trust God not only for understanding, but for guidance along the way. Obedience keeps revelation alive. It ensures that what God has shown you continues to shape who you are becoming, rather than remaining a moment you once encountered but never fully entered.

Living Revealed, Not Confused
When reflection matures into revelation, the believer no longer circles the same questions endlessly. The inner dialogue shifts. Decisions gain clarity because identity is no longer unstable. Purpose becomes visible—not always in full detail, but with enough certainty to move forward in peace.

Confusion thrives where understanding is absent. Revelation interrupts confusion by bringing divine alignment. It does not remove responsibility or challenge, but it removes inner conflict. The soul no longer wrestles with constant uncertainty because God's intention has been made clear. Scripture affirms this promise: *"For God is not the author of confusion, but of peace." 1 Corinthians 14:33*

Revelation establishes peace not by answering every question, but by settling the heart in truth. When God reveals direction, the believer no longer feels pulled in multiple directions internally. Clarity replaces hesitation. Confidence replaces inner resistance.

Living revealed means decisions are no longer driven primarily by fear, comparison, or past wounds. They are guided by understanding. The believer begins to discern what aligns with God's purpose and what distracts from it. *"The steps of a good man are ordered by the Lord: and he delighteth in his way." Psalm 37:23*

This ordering does not always feel dramatic. Often it feels steady. Revelation produces quiet confidence—the kind that does not rush, but does not retreat either. Identity also stabilizes under revelation. The believer no longer needs constant reassurance from external validation because identity is anchored in what God has revealed, not in fluctuating circumstances. *"For as many as are led by the Spirit of God, they are the sons of God." Romans 8:14*

Being led by the Spirit brings assurance. It removes the pressure to force outcomes or prove worth. When revelation leads, striving diminishes.

Revelation does not eliminate difficulty. Challenges still arise, opposition still exists, and obedience still requires courage. What revelation removes is **confusion about direction**. Believers may face resistance, but they are no longer unsure about where they are headed. *"Thy word is a lamp unto my feet, and a light unto my path." Psalm 119:105*

The Word does not illuminate the entire journey at once. It gives light for the next step. Revelation steadies the soul by providing just enough clarity to move forward without anxiety.

Living revealed means trusting God's guidance even when circumstances lag behind understanding. It means resting in alignment rather than striving for control. The heart learns to move with peace, even when outcomes remain in process. This is the fruit of revelation: not perfection, but **direction**; not certainty about everything, but **confidence in God**.

When a believer lives revealed, confusion no longer dominates the inner life. The soul becomes anchored.

The heart becomes settled. And the next step, though it may still require faith, no longer feels unclear. Revelation does not rush you. It **positions you**.

Prayer: Walking in Revelation
Father,
Thank You for what You have shown me through reflection. Now I ask for revelation that brings understanding and direction. By Your Holy Spirit, illuminate what You are doing in this season. Give me clarity that leads to obedience and peace that guards my heart as I move forward. I trust You to guide my steps, even when the full picture is not yet visible. In Jesus' name, Amen.

When reflection becomes revelation, direction is restored—and obedience becomes the natural response.

Chapter Ten
Walking in Alignment

Alignment Is a Daily Posture, Not a One-Time Decision

Alignment is not a moment you announce; it is a posture you maintain. It is not proven by what you say in a season of clarity, but by how you live once that season passes. Many believers experience powerful encounters with God—moments of revelation, clarity, or renewed commitment—but alignment is revealed in what follows afterward.

Alignment is not sustained by emotion. Emotion may initiate response, but only agreement sustains direction. When excitement fades and obedience feels ordinary, alignment is tested. It is in the quiet, repetitive choices of daily life that alignment either deepens or drifts.

Alignment means choosing, day after day, to walk in step with what God has revealed—even when obedience feels unseen, uncelebrated, or inconvenient. It is choosing faithfulness when there is no immediate affirmation and consistency when there is no emotional reinforcement.

Scripture frames alignment relationally, not mechanically: *"Can two walk together, except they be agreed?" Amos 3:3*

This verse reveals that alignment is rooted in agreement. Walking with God requires shared direction, shared values, and shared intention. Agreement precedes movement. Without agreement, movement becomes fragmented and unstable.

Alignment begins inwardly. It is the heart's decision to stay in agreement with God's truth regardless of circumstance, pressure, or delay. When circumstances shift, alignment holds. When emotions fluctuate, alignment steadies. When clarity feels distant, alignment remains committed. This is why alignment must be renewed daily. Each day presents new choices—what to prioritize, how to respond, whom to listen to, and where to invest attention. Alignment is choosing again what has already been revealed, rather than renegotiating truth based on convenience. Scripture speaks to this daily commitment: *"I beseech you therefore, brethren…that ye present your bodies a living sacrifice." Romans 12:1*

A living sacrifice is offered continually, not once. Alignment requires ongoing surrender, not a single act of dedication. Alignment also requires patience. Growth does not always feel progressive, and obedience does not always produce immediate results. Yet alignment trusts that faithfulness is never wasted, even when fruit is not yet visible. *"In due season we shall reap, if we faint not." Galatians 6:9*

Alignment keeps the believer steady during the in-between—after revelation has been given, but before fulfillment has appeared. It anchors the soul in truth rather than in outcomes.

Ultimately, alignment is choosing relationship over reaction. It is choosing to stay in agreement with God even when the path requires endurance. When alignment becomes a daily posture, obedience becomes natural, direction becomes steady, and the walk with God becomes consistent rather than conditional. Alignment is not dramatic. It is faithful.

Ordering Your Life Around Revelation
Revelation reveals direction, but alignment orders life around that direction. Many people genuinely hear God, yet struggle because their daily lives are still structured around old rhythms, old fears, or old priorities. They know what God has spoken, but their

time, energy, and attention remain arranged for a previous season.

Alignment requires intentional adjustment. It asks the believer to move beyond agreement into restructuring. Revelation without reordering creates inner tension—knowing where God is leading, yet living in a way that does not support the journey.

This may require changing how time is spent, how decisions are made, or which voices are given influence. Alignment asks difficult but necessary questions: What no longer fits where God is taking me? What habits must shift to support this new direction? What distractions am I tolerating that dilute clarity? Scripture speaks directly to this intentional ordering: *"Order my steps in thy word." Psalm 119:133*

This prayer acknowledges that direction alone is not enough. Steps must be ordered. Life must be arranged to support obedience.

The life of **Nehemiah** provides a clear example of this principle. When Nehemiah received revelation about the broken walls of Jerusalem, he did not merely feel burdened—he reordered his life around the revelation. His concern moved him to prayer, fasting, planning, and decisive action.

Nehemiah adjusted his priorities before he ever touched a stone. He rearranged his time, his focus, and even his comfort. He requested permission, gathered resources, assessed the situation carefully, and organized the people. Revelation became action because his life was reordered to support what God had revealed. *"So I came to Jerusalem…and viewed the walls." Nehemiah 2:11–13*

Nehemiah did not attempt to rebuild while maintaining an unchanged routine. The work required focus. Certain distractions had to be ignored. Certain relationships had to be discerned. Certain voices—mockery, fear, and opposition—had to lose influence.

This is what alignment looks like in practice. It is not about restriction; it is about **supporting purpose**. God rearranges what no longer serves the direction He has revealed. What once felt important may need to become secondary. What once felt optional may need to become essential.

Alignment does not remove joy; it protects it. It removes unnecessary weight so obedience can be sustained. When life is ordered around revelation, clarity increases and resistance loses power.

Nehemiah's success was not rooted in passion alone, but in alignment. His life supported the call he carried. This is the invitation of alignment—to allow God not only to speak direction, but to reshape structure. When life is ordered around revelation, obedience becomes lighter, focus becomes sharper, and purpose becomes sustainable.

Walking in the Spirit: The Key to Sustained Alignment

Alignment cannot be sustained through willpower alone. Human resolve may initiate obedience, but it cannot maintain it. Alignment requires dependence—daily, relational dependence—on the Holy Spirit. Walking in alignment is learning to respond to His promptings consistently, not only in major decisions, but in everyday attitudes, conversations, and reactions. Scripture states this plainly: *"Walk in the Spirit, and ye shall not fulfil the lust of the flesh." Galatians 5:16*

To walk in the Spirit is not to live without desire, pressure, or temptation; it is to live **led** rather than driven. It is allowing the Spirit to govern responses before impulses take control. Alignment grows when sensitivity replaces self-reliance.

The life of **Philip** provides a clear illustration of this kind of Spirit-led alignment. Philip was actively ministering in Samaria with visible fruit and momentum when the Holy Spirit redirected him—quietly and unexpectedly. *"And the angel of the Lord spake unto Philip, saying, Arise, and go toward the south."* Acts 8:26

There was no strategic explanation given. No public affirmation. No visible reward attached to the instruction. Yet Philip obeyed. He adjusted his direction not because it made sense to him, but because he was attentive to the Spirit's prompting. As Philip continued walking in obedience, the Spirit spoke again—this time with precision. *"Then the Spirit said unto Philip, Go near, and join thyself to this chariot."* Acts 8:29

This moment reveals the nature of walking in the Spirit. The Spirit did not shout. He directed. Philip did not debate. He responded. Alignment was sustained not by momentum, but by sensitivity.

Because Philip remained responsive, a divine encounter unfolded. The Ethiopian official encountered truth, understanding, and salvation—not because Philip planned it, but because Philip stayed aligned. This is what walking in the Spirit looks like in daily life. It is learning to pause before reacting. It is choosing humility in conversation. It is responding gently instead of defensively. It is allowing the Spirit to redirect tone, timing, and posture.

The Holy Spirit corrects gently, redirects quietly, and affirms faithfully. He does not force alignment; He invites it. When the believer learns to listen, adjustment becomes natural rather than disruptive. Scripture assures us that this kind of life is not chaotic, but ordered: *"For as many as are led by the Spirit of God, they are the sons of God." Romans 8:14*

Being led by the Spirit brings assurance. It removes the pressure to control outcomes and replaces it with trust. Alignment deepens because the believer is no longer relying solely on personal strength, but on divine guidance.

Walking in the Spirit is not about perfection. It is about responsiveness. It is choosing to yield quickly, adjust willingly, and trust consistently. Over time, alignment becomes less forced and more fluid. Obedience becomes lighter. Direction becomes clearer. This is the secret of sustained alignment—not trying harder, but listening better.

When sensitivity replaces self-reliance, alignment is no longer exhausting. It becomes a way of walking.

Alignment Produces Inner Peace
One of the clearest indicators of alignment is peace. This peace is not the absence of difficulty, opposition, or responsibility; it is the absence of **inner division**. When a believer is aligned with God, the heart is no longer torn between obedience and resistance, between truth and habit, or between faith and fear.

Alignment brings internal agreement. When the soul agrees with God, striving quiets. Decisions feel settled—not because they are easy, but because they are right. Even in challenging circumstances, the heart rests because it is no longer fighting direction. Scripture speaks directly to this governing role of peace: *"And let the peace of God rule in your hearts." Colossians 3:15*

The word *rule* here implies authority. Peace is not passive; it governs. It acts as an internal referee, signaling when something aligns with God's will and when it does not. When peace rules, confusion loses control. This peace is promised by Jesus Himself: *"Peace I leave with you, my peace I give unto you: not as the world giveth, give I unto you." John 14:27*

The peace God gives is not circumstantial. It is not dependent on outcomes, approval, or stability around you. It is anchored in relationship and alignment. This is why a believer can face pressure externally while remaining calm internally.

Inner conflict often reveals misalignment. When the heart feels constantly agitated, rushed, or divided, it may not be because something is difficult—it may be because something is **out of agreement**. Alignment removes this friction. It does not eliminate effort, but it eliminates resistance. Scripture reinforces this truth: *"Thou wilt keep him in perfect peace, whose mind is stayed on thee." Isaiah 26:3*

Peace is sustained when the mind remains fixed on God rather than on fear, habit, or past patterns. Alignment steadies focus. When the mind stays anchored in truth, peace follows naturally.

This does not mean every aligned decision feels comfortable. Some aligned choices stretch faith, require courage, or demand sacrifice. Yet even then, peace remains present—not because the path is painless, but because the heart knows it is walking in truth.

Peace also protects the soul from burnout. When alignment is present, obedience feels purposeful rather than draining. The believer no longer expends energy fighting God's direction or negotiating obedience internally. Peace conserves strength. Scripture affirms this protective role: *"The work of righteousness shall be peace; and the effect of righteousness quietness and assurance for ever." Isaiah 32:17*

Alignment produces peace because righteousness brings agreement with God. Where there is agreement, there is rest.

When a believer lives aligned, peace becomes more than a feeling—it becomes a **confirmation**. It reassures the heart that even when circumstances are uncertain, direction is secure. Alignment does not promise an easy path. It promises a settled heart. And a settled heart can walk forward without fear.

Consistency Over Intensity

Alignment is built through consistency, not intensity. A single powerful experience cannot sustain a life. Alignment is formed through small, faithful decisions repeated over time. This is how stability is created without burnout. Scripture affirms this principle clearly: *"He that is faithful in that which is least is faithful also in much."* Luke 16:10

Walking in alignment means showing up daily—choosing truth repeatedly, obeying in quiet ways, and remaining teachable. Calling matures through consistency, not pressure.

Correction Is Part of Alignment

Correction is not a sign of failure; it is a sign of relationship. God corrects what He is invested in. Where there is no relationship, there is no correction—only distance. Where there is covenant, correction becomes evidence of care. Scripture states this truth plainly: *"For whom the Lord loveth he correcteth; even as a father the son in whom he delighteth."* Proverbs 3:12

Correction is not punishment; it is guidance. It is not rejection; it is redirection. God does not correct to shame, but to preserve alignment. He corrects because He sees where a path is leading and intervenes before damage is done.

Alignment deepens when correction is received without offense. Offense resists growth; humility welcomes it. A heart aligned with God understands that correction protects destiny. It keeps the soul from drifting slowly away from truth while believing it is still on course. Scripture reinforces this protective role of correction: *"Moreover whom the Lord loveth he chasteneth." Hebrews 12:6*

Chastening here does not refer to harsh discipline, but to intentional training. God trains those He trusts. He adjusts what He is forming. Correction is proof that God has not given up on the process.

Correction keeps alignment honest. Without it, habits quietly replace obedience, and familiarity replaces faithfulness. Drift rarely happens suddenly; it happens gradually when small misalignments go unchecked. Correction interrupts this drift before it becomes damage.

A heart aligned with God values growth over comfort. It understands that comfort without correction produces stagnation, while correction without resistance produces maturity. Scripture affirms the fruit of correction: *"No chastening for the present seemeth to be joyous, but grievous: nevertheless afterward it yieldeth the peaceable fruit of righteousness."* Hebrews 12:11

Correction may not feel pleasant in the moment, but it produces peace later. That peace is not circumstantial—it is the peace of knowing one is walking in truth. Those who resist correction often protect comfort at the cost of direction. Those who receive correction protect purpose at the cost of pride. Alignment requires choosing purpose repeatedly, even when it requires adjustment.

Correction also sharpens discernment. The more willingly correction is received, the more quickly the heart responds to God's voice. Sensitivity increases. Delay decreases. Alignment becomes easier to maintain because the soul is no longer defensive. A heart aligned with God does not fear correction. It recognizes it as love in action. Correction does not slow your progress. It **secures your path**. And a secured path leads to lasting fruit.

Remaining Aligned in Uncertain Seasons

Not every season provides clarity. Alignment in uncertain seasons looks like trust without full visibility. It is continuing to walk forward in obedience even when outcomes remain unclear. *"Thou wilt keep him in perfect peace, whose mind is stayed on thee."* Isaiah 26:3

Alignment steadies the mind. It anchors focus on God rather than fluctuating circumstances. Even when the path feels unclear, alignment keeps the heart settled.

Alignment Requires Ongoing Surrender

Alignment is not maintained through control; it is sustained through surrender. Control attempts to secure outcomes, but surrender secures direction. Many believers lose alignment, not because they disobey God, but because they cling to what once worked instead of yielding to what God is now doing. Each season may require fresh yielding. What aligned you yesterday may need adjustment today as God continues to shape direction. God does not change His nature, but He often changes methods, timing, and emphasis. Alignment remains intact only when surrender remains active. Scripture invites the believer into this posture of trust: *"Trust in the Lord with all thine heart; and lean not unto thine own understanding." Proverbs 3:5*

This verse reveals that surrender is not passive. It is an intentional refusal to rely solely on personal understanding. Trust here is not blind—it is relational. It is confidence in God's wisdom even when the next step feels unclear.

Ongoing surrender protects the heart from rigidity. When surrender is absent, obedience can quietly turn into routine, and alignment can become mechanical. What once flowed from faith begins to flow from habit. Surrender keeps the soul responsive, teachable, and open to divine adjustment. Scripture continues this promise: *"In all thy ways acknowledge him, and he shall direct thy paths." Proverbs 3:6*

Acknowledging God "in all thy ways" implies continuous engagement. It means inviting God into decisions both large and small, planned and unexpected. This is how alignment stays alive—by remaining relational rather than procedural.

Surrender does not mean abandoning discernment or responsibility. It means releasing the need to control outcomes. It allows God to guide without resistance.

When surrender is present, correction is received without offense, redirection is accepted without fear, and waiting is endured without anxiety.

Jesus modeled this posture perfectly. Even with full authority, He surrendered daily to the Father's will. *"Not my will, but thine, be done." Luke 22:42*

This prayer reveals that surrender does not imply weakness. It demonstrates strength anchored in trust. Jesus did not surrender because He lacked power; He surrendered because He trusted the Father's purpose. Ongoing surrender also protects peace. Control breeds anxiety because it assumes responsibility God never intended you to carry. Surrender releases that burden. It returns ownership of outcomes to God while keeping the heart obedient and attentive. Alignment remains flexible when surrender remains active. A surrendered heart adjusts quickly, listens deeply, and moves freely. It does not resist change when God initiates it, and it does not cling to familiarity when God invites growth. Surrender is not losing your way. It is allowing God to lead. And when surrender becomes a daily posture, alignment is not strained—it is sustained.

Prayer: Walking in Alignment

Father,

I choose alignment with You. Order my steps according to Your Word. Where my life has been shaped by habit rather than obedience, realign me. Where fear has influenced my decisions, restore trust. Teach me to walk in step with Your Spirit daily, to remain faithful in small things, and to receive correction with humility. Let my life reflect what You have revealed. In Jesus' name, Amen.

Alignment is not a destination you arrive at—it is a posture you maintain, one faithful step at a time.

Chapter Eleven
Guarding the Image You Now See

Clarity Must Be Protected

Seeing clearly is powerful, but clarity must be guarded. Revelation without protection is vulnerable. What God restores in a season can be distorted again if it is not intentionally preserved. Clarity is a gift, but it also becomes a responsibility. Once God reveals truth, the believer is called to steward it.

Many believers receive healing, insight, and renewed identity, yet later find themselves slipping back into old patterns—not because God withdrew, but because the image was left unguarded. Old thoughts return, familiar fears resurface, and former habits attempt to reclaim influence. This regression does not mean the revelation was false; it means it was left unprotected.

The enemy rarely attacks what is broken; he targets what is becoming whole. Brokenness often keeps a person stagnant. Wholeness threatens forward movement. Once clarity appears, resistance increases—not always through obvious temptation, but through subtle erosion: distraction, doubt, fatigue, offense, or neglect.

Scripture warns us of this responsibility with sobering clarity: *"Keep thy heart with all diligence; for out of it are the issues of life."* Proverbs 4:23

The heart is the center of perception, belief, and response. What flows from your life—your words, decisions, and direction—depends on what you protect within it. Guarding the heart means guarding the clarity God has deposited there. Scripture reinforces this call to vigilance: *"Take heed unto thyself, and unto the doctrine; continue in them."* 1 Timothy 4:16

Clarity must be continued in. Truth must be revisited, rehearsed, and reinforced. Without intentional attention, even revealed truth can grow dim through neglect. The mind also plays a critical role in preserving clarity: *"Casting down imaginations, and every high thing that exalteth itself against the knowledge of God."* 2 Corinthians 10:5

Guarding clarity requires resisting thoughts that contradict what God has revealed. Old narratives must be confronted, not entertained. When the mind is left unguarded, clarity in the heart can be compromised. Scripture further exhorts believers to remain alert: *"Be sober, be vigilant."* 1 Peter 5:8

Vigilance does not mean fear; it means awareness. It is recognizing that clarity must be maintained intentionally. Revelation creates responsibility. Insight requires stewardship.

Clarity is preserved through prayer, the Word, discernment, and obedience. It is guarded by renewing the mind, choosing life-giving environments, and staying sensitive to the Holy Spirit. What God reveals must be valued enough to protect. Clarity does not fade because God changes. It fades when it is no longer guarded.

What you protect will continue to shape you. What you neglect may slowly distort again. Guard the clarity God has given you—it is guiding you toward who you are becoming.

Why the Enemy Targets Identity After Revelation

The moment identity becomes clear, opposition becomes strategic. Revelation shifts spiritual posture. It moves a believer from confusion into alignment, from passivity into purpose. Because of this, identity becomes the primary target after revelation—not circumstances, not possessions, not even opportunity, but **agreement**.

The enemy understands something many believers overlook: if identity can be distorted, direction will follow. Obedience weakens when identity is questioned. Confidence erodes when truth is challenged. This is why the enemy's strategy often intensifies **after** God has spoken clearly. Scripture reveals the enemy's intent plainly: *"The thief cometh not, but for to steal, and to kill, and to destroy."* John 10:10

The enemy steals first—not peace, not joy, but **truth**. He attempts to steal what God has revealed before it can fully take root.

This pattern is seen clearly in the life of **Satan**'s interaction with Jesus. Immediately after Jesus' baptism, where the Father publicly affirmed His identity, the Spirit led Him into the wilderness. *"This is my beloved Son, in whom I am well pleased."* Matthew 3:17

The enemy's first words in the wilderness were not about hunger, power, or authority—they were about identity. *"If thou be the Son of God..."* Matthew 4:3

The enemy did not deny Jesus' power; he questioned His identity. This reveals a critical truth: **identity affirmed by God will be challenged by the enemy**.

The enemy does not need to remove the revelation—he only needs to introduce doubt about it.

After revelation, the enemy often works subtly. He does not always attack with obvious temptation. Instead, he uses erosion:
- doubt disguised as logic
- comparison disguised as discernment
- weariness disguised as wisdom
- offense disguised as self-respect

Scripture warns believers to remain aware of this subtlety: *"For we wrestle not against flesh and blood." Ephesians 6:12*

The battle is not external first; it is internal. Identity is challenged in the mind before it ever affects behavior. This is why Scripture also exhorts believers to guard their thinking: *"Be sober, be vigilant; because your adversary the devil…seeketh whom he may devour." 1 Peter 5:8*

Vigilance here does not mean fear. It means awareness. The enemy seeks opportunity where identity is unguarded. He looks for moments of fatigue, isolation, disappointment, or neglect—times when clarity is present but not reinforced.

The enemy understands that **broken people are not the greatest threat**. He targets those who are becoming whole, because wholeness produces movement. Identity produces authority. Authority disrupts deception. Scripture affirms this authority: *"And they overcame him by the blood of the Lamb, and by the word of their testimony." Revelation 12:11*

Testimony is identity spoken aloud. It is agreement with what God has revealed. When testimony is silenced or doubted internally, authority weakens. This is why guarding identity after revelation is essential. Truth must be rehearsed. The Word must be spoken. Agreement must be maintained. Jesus did not argue with the enemy; He answered with Scripture. He reinforced identity with truth, not emotion. *"It is written…" Matthew 4:4*

Identity is preserved by agreement with God's Word. The enemy targets identity after revelation because identity determines obedience. When identity is secure, obedience is natural. When identity is shaken, obedience becomes negotiable. Revelation is powerful—but **revelation unguarded becomes vulnerable**. This is why Scripture urges believers to remain rooted: *"That we henceforth be no more children, tossed to and fro." Ephesians 4:14*

Stability follows maturity. Guarded identity produces steadiness. The enemy does not fear information. He fears **transformation**. And transformation begins when identity is revealed and protected. Guard the image God has shown you—it is the foundation of everything that follows.

Renewing the Mind to Preserve the Image
What God reveals in the spirit must be protected in the mind. Revelation may restore identity, but the mind determines whether that identity is preserved or slowly distorted again. This is why renewing the mind is not a secondary discipline—it is a primary safeguard. Scripture is clear that transformation is sustained through renewal, not memory alone: *"And be not conformed to this world: but be ye transformed by the renewing of your mind." Romans 12:2*

Transformation does not remain intact without renewal. Old thought patterns do not disappear automatically when truth is revealed. They must be intentionally replaced. Without renewal, the mind will default to familiarity, even if familiarity contradicts truth.

Many believers lose clarity, not because God stopped speaking, but because they stopped renewing. They received revelation, but continued to think from old narratives—fear, insecurity, rejection, comparison, or self-doubt. Over time, those thoughts begin to blur the image God restored.

Renewing the mind means actively aligning thoughts with what God has revealed, not with what experience once taught. It is choosing truth repeatedly until it becomes the dominant voice within. Scripture emphasizes this internal responsibility: *"For as he thinketh in his heart, so is he." Proverbs 23:7*

Identity follows thought. If the mind rehearses lies, the heart begins to live as though those lies are true—even after revelation. This is why guarding clarity requires discipline at the level of thinking. The apostle Paul gives practical instruction for this process: *"Casting down imaginations, and every high thing that exalteth itself against the knowledge of God." 2 Corinthians 10:5*

Not every thought deserves agreement. Renewing the mind involves discernment—recognizing which thoughts align with God's revealed image and which oppose it. Thoughts that contradict what God has spoken must be confronted, not entertained.

Renewal also requires consistency. The mind is shaped by repetition. What is rehearsed becomes familiar, and what becomes familiar begins to feel true. This is why Scripture meditation is essential after revelation. *"This book of the law shall not depart out of thy mouth; but thou shalt meditate therein day and night." Joshua 1:8*

Meditation reinforces revelation. It anchors truth deeply enough that it resists erosion. When the Word becomes familiar, lies lose power. Renewing the mind also protects the heart from emotional regression. Emotions often follow thoughts. When the mind is renewed, emotions gradually align. Peace replaces anxiety. Confidence replaces fear. Stability replaces confusion. Scripture assures us of this protection: *"And the peace of God, which passeth all understanding, shall keep your hearts and minds." Philippians 4:7*

Notice that peace guards both heart and mind. Renewed thinking creates an environment where peace can rule. Renewing the mind is not about striving for perfection. It is about consistency. It is choosing daily to agree with God's truth over past experience, present emotion, or external pressure. The image God reveals is preserved where the mind is renewed. Without renewal, revelation fades into memory. With renewal, revelation matures into lifestyle.

Guard your thinking. It is the doorway through which clarity either remains—or slowly escapes.

Guarding Your Words
Words are powerful carriers of image. What God restores internally must be reinforced verbally. After revelation, the mouth becomes a gate—either protecting truth or reopening old agreements. This is why guarding your words is essential to preserving clarity. Scripture makes this responsibility unmistakably clear: *"Death and life are in the power of the tongue." Proverbs 18:21*

Words do not merely express thoughts; they **shape belief**. What is spoken repeatedly begins to feel true, even when it contradicts what God has revealed. Many believers lose clarity not because revelation failed, but because their words quietly dismantled it.

After God restores identity, careless speech can reopen doors that revelation closed. Speaking from fear, frustration, or fatigue may feel harmless, yet it often revives old narratives—*I'm not enough, I always fail, nothing changes.* These words are not neutral. They reinforce images God has already corrected. Scripture warns against this subtle danger: *"A wholesome tongue is a tree of life: but perverseness therein is a breach in the spirit." Proverbs 15:4*

Words either nourish the spirit or fracture it. Guarding your words is not about denying struggle; it is about refusing to let struggle redefine truth. You can acknowledge difficulty without speaking defeat. Jesus Himself modeled this discipline. When tested in the wilderness, He did not argue emotionally or speak impulsively. He responded with truth. *"It is written…" Matthew 4:4*

Jesus guarded His identity with His words. He did not explain Himself. He reinforced what had already been spoken by the Father. This teaches us that words aligned with Scripture are defensive tools against distortion. Scripture further instructs believers to be intentional with speech: *"Let no corrupt communication proceed out of your mouth, but that which is good to the use of edifying." Ephesians 4:29*

Edifying speech builds what God is forming. It strengthens identity rather than weakening it. Guarding your words means choosing language that agrees with God's truth—even when emotions are unsettled. This does not mean pretending pain does not exist. It means refusing to give pain authority over identity. You can say, *"This is hard,"* without saying, *"I am defeated."* You can say, *"I am still healing,"* without saying, *"I am broken."* Jesus explained why this matters: *"For out of the abundance of the heart the mouth speaketh." Matthew 12:34*

Words reveal what the heart is agreeing with. Guarding your words, then, also guards the heart. When speech aligns with revelation, belief stabilizes and clarity remains intact. Over time, guarded speech retrains the inner world. Faith grows. Peace increases. Old lies lose strength. The image God revealed becomes familiar rather than fragile. Guarding your words is not about silence—it is about **alignment**. Speak what God has spoken. Reinforce what He has revealed. Protect the image by protecting the language that shapes it. What you consistently speak, you consistently strengthen. And what you strengthen will shape who you become.

Choosing Environment Wisely

Environment is never neutral. What surrounds you continually speaks to you, shapes you, and reinforces what you believe about yourself. After revelation, choosing environment wisely becomes essential, because clarity is either strengthened or slowly diluted by what you allow to influence you.

Many believers underestimate the power of environment. They guard their thoughts and words, yet remain immersed in spaces that contradict what God has revealed. Over time, these environments quietly erode clarity—not through confrontation, but through familiarity. Scripture warns us clearly: *"Be not deceived: evil communications corrupt good manners."* 1 Corinthians 15:33

This verse does not refer only to immoral behavior. It speaks to influence—conversations, attitudes, values, and perspectives that subtly shape thinking. Environment includes people, media, routines, atmospheres, and even unspoken expectations. After God restores identity, certain environments may no longer fit. This does not mean rejection of people; it means discernment of influence. Jesus Himself withdrew regularly—not because He lacked love, but because He valued alignment.

"And he withdrew himself into the wilderness, and prayed."
Luke 5:16

Withdrawal can be strategic. It creates space for clarity to deepen and for alignment to remain intact. The life of Abraham illustrates this principle clearly. God did not only call Abraham to a promise; He called him to leave an environment that could limit obedience. *"Get thee out of thy country, and from thy kindred, and from thy father's house." Genesis 12:1*

God understood that environment shapes expectation. Remaining in familiar surroundings could have constrained Abraham's ability to trust what God was revealing. Leaving was not punishment—it was protection.

Choosing environment wisely also means recognizing seasons. Some environments may be appropriate at one stage and restrictive at another. Growth often requires reassessment. What once supported healing may later hinder maturity. Scripture encourages intentional association: *"He that walketh with wise men shall be wise." Proverbs 13:20*

Wisdom multiplies in the right environment. Alignment strengthens when surrounded by voices that reinforce truth, encourage obedience, and honor growth. Environment also includes what you repeatedly consume—conversations, content, music, and information. These inputs shape inner dialogue. If they contradict revelation, clarity weakens over time. Scripture exhorts believers to choose deliberately: *"Finally, brethren, whatsoever things are true… think on these things." Philippians 4:8*

Choosing environment wisely is not about isolation or superiority. It is about stewardship. You are responsible for what influences you after God has revealed truth. Environment does not define you—but it does **train** you. When environment aligns with revelation, growth accelerates. When it contradicts revelation, confusion slowly returns. Choosing environment wisely protects the image God has restored. It allows clarity to deepen, peace to remain, and obedience to stay sustainable.

Not every door needs to stay open. Not every voice needs continued access. Not every space supports who you are becoming. Wisdom knows when to remain—and when to move.

Jesus: Guarding Identity in the Wilderness

Jesus Himself modeled how identity must be guarded immediately after revelation. Following His baptism—where the Father publicly affirmed who He was—Jesus was led into the wilderness. This timing is significant. Revelation was followed by testing, not celebration. *"This is my beloved Son, in whom I am well pleased." Matthew 3:17*

The affirmation was clear, complete, and sufficient. Nothing was missing. Yet the wilderness revealed that affirmation must be **defended**, not merely received. The enemy's first attack was not on Jesus' power, gifting, or authority. It was on His identity. *"If thou be the Son of God…" Matthew 4:3* That single word—*if*—was an attempt to reopen what God had already settled. The enemy did not try to make Jesus someone else; he tried to make Jesus **question who He already was**. This reveals a vital truth: identity affirmed by God will often be challenged by doubt, especially in isolated or vulnerable seasons.

Jesus did not respond emotionally. He did not defend Himself. He did not explain His calling or rehearse His baptism. He responded with truth. *"It is written …" Matthew 4:4* Jesus guarded the image by reinforcing what God had already spoken. He anchored identity in Scripture rather than circumstance. Hunger, isolation, and pressure did not alter His response because His agreement with the Father was settled.

This teaches us that identity must be defended with truth, not emotion. Feelings fluctuate, but truth remains constant. When identity is questioned, the appropriate response is not argument, but alignment. Not explanation, but agreement with the Word.
Jesus' example shows that guarding identity is not loud or dramatic. It is firm, quiet, and rooted. He did not strive to prove His sonship; He rested in it.

After revelation comes testing—but testing does not mean revelation was false. It means revelation was **important**. Guarding identity after revelation ensures that what God has spoken remains authoritative, even in the wilderness. Truth spoken by God does not need to be defended emotionally. It only needs to be **reinforced faithfully**. And when identity is guarded this way, purpose remains intact.

Rest as a Guardrail
Fatigue weakens discernment. Many believers lose clarity not through sin, rebellion, or compromise, but through exhaustion. When the soul is tired,

boundaries blur. When the body is depleted, the mind becomes vulnerable. Rest, therefore, is not laziness; it is protection.

Exhaustion has a way of distorting perception. What once felt clear begins to feel confusing. What once felt manageable begins to feel overwhelming. In these moments, believers may question what God has already settled—not because truth has changed, but because strength has been drained. Scripture acknowledges this human reality: *"He giveth power to the faint; and to them that have no might he increaseth strength." Isaiah 40:29*

God strengthens, but He also invites rest as part of His design. Strength is renewed, not manufactured. Even Jesus—fully aware of His mission and fully submitted to the Father—withdrew intentionally to rest and pray. He did not equate constant activity with faithfulness. He recognized the necessity of withdrawal to preserve clarity. *"Come ye yourselves apart into a desert place, and rest a while." Mark 6:31*

This invitation came after ministry, not before failure. Jesus understood that rest was required **to sustain alignment**, not to recover from wrongdoing. Rest was a guardrail that protected both His disciples' strength and their discernment. Scripture further reveals Jesus' rhythm: *"And he withdrew himself into the wilderness, and prayed." Luke 5:16*

Withdrawal was not avoidance; it was alignment. Jesus stepped away to remain centered in the Father's will. He rested to preserve clarity, not to escape responsibility.

Guarding the image God has restored includes honoring physical, emotional, and spiritual rhythms that sustain clarity. Sleep, stillness, silence, and prayer are not optional luxuries—they are spiritual safeguards. When these rhythms are neglected, even truth can feel heavy and obedience can feel burdensome.

The enemy often exploits fatigue because exhaustion lowers resistance. Discernment dulls when rest is ignored. This is why Scripture calls believers to intentional care: *"Be careful for nothing… and the peace of God… shall keep your hearts and minds." Philippians 4:6–7*

Peace guards the mind, but peace is often sustained through rest. Rest also restores perspective. It allows the heart to settle and the mind to realign with truth.

In rest, God recalibrates what has been strained by constant output. Scripture offers this gentle promise: *"Come unto me, all ye that labour and are heavy laden, and I will give you rest." Matthew 11:28* This rest is not merely physical—it is soul rest. It is the restoration of clarity, trust, and alignment. A rested believer discerns more clearly. A rested heart hears more accurately. A rested mind resists distortion more effectively. Rest does not slow purpose. It **preserves** it. When rest becomes a guardrail, clarity remains protected, identity stays anchored, and obedience becomes sustainable. Honor rest. It is part of how God guards what He has restored.

Staying Submitted to the Holy Spirit

Ultimately, the Holy Spirit is the guardian of revelation. What God reveals through the Word and through seasons of encounter is preserved through ongoing submission to the Spirit. He does not only illuminate truth in moments of insight; He sustains it through daily guidance, gentle correction, and continual re-centering. Scripture affirms this role clearly: *"Howbeit when he, the Spirit of truth, is come, he will guide you into all truth." John 16:13*

Notice that the Spirit *guides*. Guidance implies movement, direction, and relationship. The Holy

Spirit does not simply deposit truth and withdraw; He walks with the believer to ensure that truth remains active, accurate, and applied.

Staying submitted to the Holy Spirit keeps the image God has revealed alive. Submission allows the Spirit to remind the heart of what God has spoken when distraction, pressure, or fatigue attempt to blur clarity. He brings truth back into focus—not with condemnation, but with reassurance. Jesus promised this function explicitly: *"But the Comforter, which is the Holy Ghost… he shall teach you all things, and bring all things to your remembrance." John 14:26*

The Spirit reminds because revelation can be forgotten. He re-centers because alignment can drift. Drift is rarely intentional; it is often gradual. Submission allows the Spirit to interrupt drift before it becomes distance. The Holy Spirit also corrects—not harshly, but precisely. Correction from the Spirit is relational, not punitive. It feels like conviction, not accusation. It redirects the heart without crushing it. Scripture confirms this inner witness: *"As many as are led by the Spirit of God, they are the sons of God." Romans 8:14* Being led by the Spirit is evidence of relationship and maturity. Submission keeps the believer teachable, responsive, and aware. It allows

God to adjust posture, attitude, and direction without resistance. Staying submitted also protects against self-deception. Even sincere believers can begin to rely on past revelation without present guidance. Submission keeps revelation current. It ensures that what God revealed then is applied rightly now.

The Spirit preserves truth by maintaining alignment between revelation and obedience. *"Grieve not the holy Spirit of God." Ephesians 4:30* This warning reminds us that resistance dulls sensitivity. Submission sharpens it. When the Spirit is honored, His voice becomes clearer and His guidance more trusted.

Submission does not mean losing discernment or responsibility. It means yielding the need to control. It allows God to lead without interruption. A submitted heart remains flexible, humble, and responsive—able to adjust quickly when the Spirit signals correction or redirection.

The Spirit does not only reveal truth—He preserves it. He guards the image God has restored. He keeps clarity from fading into memory. When the believer stays submitted, truth remains living, identity remains stable, and direction remains sure.

Submission is not weakness. It is wisdom that keeps revelation alive.

Prayer: Guarding What God Has Restored
Father,
Thank You for restoring clarity, identity, and truth in my life. Teach me to guard what You have revealed. Help me to renew my mind daily, to speak in agreement with Your Word, and to choose environments that reinforce growth. Strengthen me to resist distortion and to remain anchored in truth. I trust You to preserve what You have restored. In Jesus' name, Amen.

What God has revealed is precious—guard it carefully, and it will continue to shape who you are becoming.

Chapter Twelve
Living from the True Image

From Protection to Expression

Guarding the image is essential, but it is not the final goal. Protection is a season, not a destination. The purpose of guarding what God has restored is not preservation alone—it is **expression**. God did not restore your identity so that you would live cautiously, hesitantly, or constantly self-monitoring. He restored it so that you would live **confidently, freely, and authentically from truth**.

Living from the true image means the believer no longer relates to life through wounds, distortions, or old narratives. Decisions are no longer filtered through fear, insecurity, or self-doubt. Instead of reacting from pain, the believer responds from alignment. Life is no longer approached defensively, but **anchored in assurance**. Scripture describes this freedom with clarity: *"If the Son therefore shall make you free, ye shall be free indeed." John 8:36*

This freedom is not the absence of responsibility. It is not permission to wander or live without boundaries. It is empowerment—the ability to live authentically without fear of losing identity. Freedom means you no longer have to protect yourself from life because your identity is no longer fragile. When a believer lives from the true image, obedience flows naturally. Confidence replaces hesitation. Peace replaces striving. The heart is no longer asking, *"Am I enough?"* because that question has already been answered by God.

The life of **Peter** after his restoration illustrates this transformation clearly. Before the cross, Peter's identity was unstable. Though called, he often acted from insecurity, fear, and impulse. His denial of Jesus was not simply a failure of courage—it was a reflection of an identity that had not yet been fully healed. After the denial, Peter withdrew. Shame silenced him. Fear shaped his behavior.

But after the resurrection, Jesus restored Peter—not by revisiting failure repeatedly, but by re-establishing identity and calling. *"Simon, son of Jonas, lovest thou me?" John 21:16*

Jesus did not ask Peter to prove himself. He invited Peter to live from love rather than from regret. With each affirmation, Jesus repositioned Peter—not as a man defined by denial, but as one entrusted with responsibility. From that moment on, Peter no longer lived from fear. He lived from restored identity. In the book of Acts, the same Peter who once denied Jesus now stood boldly, speaking with authority and clarity. *"Then Peter, filled with the Holy Ghost, said…" Acts 4:8*

Peter was no longer guarding himself; he was **expressing who he had become**. He was not trying to prove loyalty—he was living from it. His words carried authority because they flowed from alignment, not insecurity. This is what it means to live from the true image.

You stop rehearsing who you were and begin expressing who God says you are. You stop shrinking to stay safe and start standing because you are secure. You no longer measure every step out of fear of failure; you move with peace because identity is settled.

Living from the true image does not mean life becomes effortless. It means effort is no longer fueled by fear. It means service flows from wholeness, not from striving. It means obedience is joyful rather than exhausting. Freedom here is not recklessness—it is **confidence rooted in truth**. It is the ability to live openly, love deeply, speak boldly, and obey faithfully without the constant need for self-protection. When identity is healed and guarded, it no longer needs to be defended. It is simply **lived**. And when a believer lives from the true image, life stops feeling like something to manage carefully and becomes something to **express faithfully**—to the glory of God.

Identity as a Foundation, Not a Question
When identity is healed, revealed, and guarded, it no longer functions as a question—it becomes a foundation. The believer no longer approaches life asking, *"Who am I?"* every time pressure arises. Identity has been settled in God, and from that place, life is built rather than negotiated.

A questioned identity produces instability. Decisions become reactive. Emotions fluctuate easily. Confidence rises and falls based on outcomes or opinions. But when identity becomes a foundation, the inner world stabilizes. The believer no longer measures worth by performance or approval, but by truth already established. Scripture describes this settled position clearly: *"For ye are dead, and your life is hid with Christ in God." Colossians 3:3*

When life is hidden with Christ, identity is secure. It is no longer exposed to every challenge, delay, or critique. The believer does not need to defend who they are, because God has already defined it.

Identity as a foundation changes how pressure is handled. Correction can be received without collapse. Delay can be endured without self-doubt. Opposition can be faced without panic. When identity is not in question, circumstances lose the power to redefine the soul. Scripture affirms this stability: *"Being rooted and built up in him, and stablished in the faith." Colossians 2:7* Roots do not ask who they are when the wind blows. They hold.

The life of **Daniel** offers a powerful illustration of identity as foundation. Daniel lived in a foreign culture, under pressure to assimilate, compromise, and redefine himself according to new systems. Yet Daniel did not debate who he was. His identity was settled long before he was tested. *"But Daniel purposed in his heart that he would not defile himself." Daniel 1:8*

Notice the language—*purposed in his heart*. Daniel did not wait until the pressure came to decide who he was. His identity was already established. Because of this,

his obedience was calm, not confrontational. He did not resist loudly; he stood quietly.

As pressure increased—from dietary compromise to threats of death—Daniel's identity remained unmoved. When faced with the lion's den, he did not negotiate his faith or question God's presence. *"My God hath sent his angel, and hath shut the lions' mouths." Daniel 6:22*

Daniel's confidence flowed from identity, not circumstance. He lived from who he knew he was in God, not from fear of consequence. This is the fruit of identity as foundation. The believer no longer lives in constant self-assessment. They live in agreement. Decisions are made from truth rather than from insecurity. Obedience is steady because it is not fueled by fear. Scripture assures believers of this grounding: *"For other foundation can no man lay than that is laid, which is Jesus Christ." 1 Corinthians 3:11*

When Christ is the foundation, identity does not shift with seasons. Growth continues. Maturity deepens. Confidence becomes quiet and unshakeable. Living with identity as a foundation means you no longer need to prove who you are—you simply **build from it**. You serve from security. You lead from assurance.

You endure from peace. Identity is no longer a question asked under pressure. It is a foundation that holds under weight. And when identity is settled, life becomes less about self-protection and more about faithful expression.

Living Authentically Without Apology
One of the clearest signs that identity has been restored is the ability to live authentically without apology. Authenticity does not mean carelessness or self-centeredness; it means alignment. It is the freedom to live honestly before God and others without shrinking, pretending, or performing to be accepted.

When identity is unsettled, people apologize for who they are. They mute their convictions, dilute their gifts, or reshape their voice to fit expectations. But when identity is healed, believers no longer feel the need to explain, defend, or justify their God-given design. Life is lived from truth rather than approval. Scripture affirms this confidence: *"Am I now seeking the approval of man, or of God?" Galatians 1:10*

Authenticity is not rebellion against people; it is allegiance to God. When the believer's primary agreement is with God, secondary voices lose their power to define worth.

Living authentically also releases peace. There is no longer an inner conflict between who you are and how you live. The believer no longer alternates between masks—one for faith, one for survival, one for acceptance. Integrity replaces fragmentation. *"Let your conversation be without covetousness; and be content with such things as ye have." Hebrews 13:5*

Contentment here reflects internal alignment. It is the quiet assurance that you do not need to become someone else to be effective or loved.

The life of **Esther** illustrates this kind of authenticity powerfully. Esther initially concealed her identity out of necessity and wisdom, but there came a moment when hiding was no longer aligned with God's purpose. Living authentically became an act of obedience. *"And who knoweth whether thou art come to the kingdom for such a time as this?" Esther 4:14*

When Esther chose to reveal who she truly was, she did so without apology. She did not demand permission to be herself. She aligned with purpose, even though the cost was high. *"If I perish, I perish."* *Esther 4:16*

This statement was not resignation; it was clarity. Esther lived from identity rather than fear. Her authenticity carried authority because it flowed from obedience.

Living authentically without apology does not mean living loudly. It often looks quiet, consistent, and unforced. Confidence becomes steady rather than performative. The believer no longer competes for validation or compares calling. Scripture encourages this freedom: *"Stand fast therefore in the liberty wherewith Christ hath made us free." Galatians 5:1*

Authenticity is a form of liberty. It allows the believer to occupy space fully, love sincerely, and serve faithfully without self-negotiation. When you live authentically, you give others permission to do the same. Your life becomes a testimony, not of perfection, but of alignment. You reflect Christ not by imitation, but by incarnation—truth lived out through a healed identity. Living authentically without apology means:
- You speak truth without harshness.
- You set boundaries without guilt.

- You obey God without explanation.
- You walk confidently without comparison.

Authenticity is not arrogance. It is agreement with who God says you are. When identity is settled, apology is no longer required for obedience. You simply live — fully, faithfully, and free.

Authority Flows from Identity
Spiritual authority does not begin with position, title, or visibility. It begins with identity. When identity is settled in God, authority flows naturally. It does not need to be announced, proven, or defended. It is recognized because it is rooted in truth. Authority that is not anchored in identity becomes performative. It strives to impress rather than influence. But authority that flows from identity carries weight because it flows from alignment, not ambition. Scripture reveals this principle clearly in the life of Jesus: *"For he taught them as one having authority, and not as the scribes." Matthew 7:29*

Jesus' authority did not come from institutional approval or public validation. It came from knowing who He was and whose He was. He spoke with authority because He lived from identity, not insecurity.

Authority flows most freely when identity is no longer questioned. When a believer is unsure of who they are, they hesitate. They over-explain. They seek affirmation before obedience. But when identity is established, obedience becomes confident and authority becomes evident. Scripture confirms this internal grounding: *"And Jesus knowing that the Father had given all things into his hands…he rose." John 13:3–4*

Notice the sequence. Jesus **knew** who He was before He acted. Identity preceded authority in action. Because His identity was secure, even acts of humility carried authority.

This same pattern is visible in the life of **David**. David did not receive authority when he became king; authority was already forming when he was still a shepherd. His confidence before Goliath was not rooted in size, status, or experience—it was rooted in identity. *"The Lord that delivered me out of the paw of the lion…he will deliver me." 1 Samuel 17:37*

David did not borrow Saul's armor because it did not fit who he was. Authority flowed from authenticity. He fought as who he was, not who others expected him to be.

When identity is settled, authority expresses itself through obedience, clarity, and peace. Prayer becomes confident. Discernment sharpens. Decisions carry weight because they are made from agreement with God. Scripture affirms this promise to believers: *"Behold, I give unto you power… and nothing shall by any means hurt you." Luke 10:19*

This power is not reckless or domineering. It is exercised through submission to God and confidence in truth. Authority that flows from identity does not dominate—it **serves**, **leads**, and **establishes order**. Authority also manifests through restraint. When identity is secure, the believer does not react impulsively or defend unnecessarily. Silence can carry as much authority as speech. Stillness can be stronger than striving. Scripture reminds us: *"The Lord shall fight for you, and ye shall hold your peace." Exodus 14:14*

Authority flows where trust replaces control. When a believer lives from restored identity, authority becomes consistent rather than situational. It does not rise and fall with emotions or circumstances. It is expressed quietly, confidently, and effectively. Authority is not loud confidence. It is settled agreement with God.

When identity is healed, authority follows naturally. You no longer try to carry it — **it carries you**.

Living from Rest, Not Striving
When identity is healed and authority is established, the believer is invited into a new posture—**rest**. This rest is not inactivity or disengagement; it is freedom from striving. Striving is the effort to secure what God has already promised. Rest is the confidence that what God has spoken does not need to be forced.

Many believers are faithful, disciplined, and committed—yet exhausted. Their weariness does not come from obedience, but from striving to prove worth, accelerate outcomes, or control results. Living from rest means obedience flows from trust rather than anxiety. Scripture invites the believer into this posture: *"Come unto me, all ye that labour and are heavy laden, and I will give you rest."* Matthew 11:28

This rest is not merely physical. It is rest for the soul—the place where pressure lifts and identity no longer feels fragile. When the soul rests, obedience becomes lighter and direction clearer. Living from rest means the believer no longer measures effectiveness by constant activity. Faithfulness replaces frantic effort. The believer understands that

God works most powerfully through alignment, not exhaustion. *"For he that is entered into his rest, he also hath ceased from his own works."* Hebrews 4:10

Ceasing from one's own works does not mean ceasing from God's work. It means releasing the need to perform for approval or rush for security. Rest shifts the source of effort—from self to God.

The story of **Mary** and **Martha** illustrates this contrast clearly. Both loved Jesus. Both desired to honor Him. Yet one operated from striving, the other from rest. Martha was busy, distracted, and overwhelmed by responsibility. Mary, however, chose stillness and presence. *"But one thing is needful: and Mary hath chosen that good part."* Luke 10:42

Mary's rest was not laziness—it was alignment. She positioned herself to receive rather than rush. Jesus affirmed that rest rooted in relationship produces what striving cannot. Striving often disguises itself as diligence, but it is driven by fear of lack, fear of delay, or fear of insignificance. Rest, by contrast, is driven by trust. It believes God is faithful even when progress feels slow. Scripture assures us of this stability: *"Thou wilt keep him in perfect peace, whose mind is stayed on thee."* Isaiah 26:3

Peace is a byproduct of rest. When the mind is anchored in God rather than in outcomes, striving dissolves.

Living from rest also sharpens discernment. Decisions are no longer rushed. Reactions are no longer impulsive. The believer moves with clarity rather than compulsion. *"In returning and rest shall ye be saved; in quietness and in confidence shall be your strength." Isaiah 30:15*

Strength flows from rest, not strain. When identity is settled, rest becomes possible. When authority is rooted in trust, striving becomes unnecessary. The believer learns to work diligently without anxiety, to wait without fear, and to obey without pressure. Living from rest does not slow purpose. It **sustains** it. Rest does not weaken obedience. It **purifies** it. When a believer lives from rest rather than striving, life is no longer something to chase—it becomes something to steward calmly, confidently, and faithfully in God.

Becoming a Living Reflection
When identity is restored and lived from, the believer becomes a reflection of Christ to others—not

through effort, but through presence. Transformation matures beyond internal healing and begins to express itself externally, not by force, but by overflow. The life itself begins to speak. Scripture describes this transformation with holy clarity: *"But we all, with open face beholding as in a glass the glory of the Lord, are changed into the same image." 2 Corinthians 3:18*

This change is not cosmetic; it is progressive and inward. As the believer continues to behold Christ, likeness emerges naturally. Reflection happens not by striving to imitate, but by staying near. Proximity produces resemblance.

Becoming a living reflection means others begin to encounter healing, clarity, and peace not because of what you explain, but because of who you have become. The atmosphere around your life shifts. Your presence carries calm. Your words carry weight. Your responses carry grace. Scripture affirms this quiet influence: *"Ye are the light of the world." Matthew 5:14*

Light does not announce itself—it illuminates. In the same way, a believer living from restored identity does not attempt to impress or persuade. Truth becomes visible through consistency, humility, and love.

The life of **Stephen** illustrates this reality powerfully. Stephen did not perform miracles to prove his faith. He did not campaign for influence. Yet Scripture records something remarkable about his presence: *"And all that sat in the council… saw his face as it had been the face of an angel." Acts 6:15*

Stephen's reflection was not a strategy—it was the result of alignment. Even in opposition, his countenance revealed peace and conviction. His life bore witness before his words ever did.

Becoming a living reflection also means releasing the need to be understood by everyone. Reflection does not require explanation. The believer learns that transformation speaks louder than testimony alone. People recognize authenticity without needing it to be defended. Scripture reminds us: *"By this shall all men know that ye are my disciples, if ye have love one to another." John 13:35*

Love, peace, and truth lived consistently become unmistakable markers of Christlikeness.

A living reflection does not strive for visibility. It simply remains faithful. It listens well. It responds gently. It walks steadily. Over time, the image becomes evident—not because the believer tried to display it, but because they remained aligned with the One they behold. When identity is healed and authority is settled, reflection becomes effortless. The believer no longer asks how to represent Christ; representation becomes natural.

You do not reflect Christ by trying harder. You reflect Christ by staying close. And as you live from the true image, your life becomes a mirror—quietly revealing the glory of the One who restored you.

Prayer: Living from the True Image
Father,
I thank You for restoring my identity and aligning my heart with truth. Teach me now to live from what You have revealed. Help me to walk in authenticity, peace, and confidence rooted in You. Let my life reflect Your image without striving or fear. I choose to live from truth, not from distortion. In Jesus' name, Amen.

When you live from the true image God has revealed, life no longer feels like something to survive—it becomes something to steward with confidence and peace.

Chapter Thirteen
Leaving the Old Image Behind

Release Is Required for Permanence

Restoration reveals the true image. Alignment teaches you how to live from it. But permanence requires one final act: **release**. The old image—formed by pain, fear, survival, rejection, betrayal, or distortion—must be intentionally left behind. Not revisited. Not negotiated with. Not occasionally entertained. Because anything you keep revisiting, you keep giving access to.

Many believers love God sincerely and have experienced real healing, yet they still glance backward. They have clarity, but they keep references to who they used to be. They keep old labels in their vocabulary. They keep old reactions as "default settings." They keep old expectations about life that are rooted in former disappointment. This creates unnecessary tension, because it forces the soul to live between two identities: the one God restored, and the one history once formed. Release is what ends that tension. Scripture speaks directly to this transition: *"Remember ye not the former things, neither consider the things of old." Isaiah 43:18*

God does not say the former things never happened. He says they no longer define direction. He is not denying history; He is removing its authority. This verse is not about amnesia—it is about leadership. God is saying, "Do not let what was become the reference point for what is." Because the danger of the old image is not only in what it did to you—it is in what it keeps telling you about you. The old image whispers familiar sentences in the mind: *This is how life always goes. This is what people always do. This is what I always become.* And if those whispers are entertained, they become agreements again. That is why release must be intentional.

Release means you stop using old pain as your identity language. You stop introducing yourself through what wounded you. You stop interpreting new seasons through old disappointments. You stop expecting God to repeat what He has already healed. You stop assuming that what happened before must happen again. Release also means you stop rehearsing the old story as though it is still the current truth. Some believers are healed, but they keep narrating from the wound. They have been restored, but they keep speaking from the fracture. They are no longer bound, but they keep thinking like captives. Scripture addresses this pattern clearly: *"As a man thinketh in his heart, so is he." Proverbs 23:7*

If the mind remains attached to the old image, the life will keep expressing it—even after healing has begun. This is why permanence requires a decision. Healing reveals truth, but release establishes it. Release is not pretending the past did not hurt. It is refusing to let pain become your identity. It is acknowledging what happened without letting it set your future boundaries. It is honoring what you survived without staying shaped by it.

In many cases, the old image returns during pressure. When you are tired, offended, discouraged, or misunderstood, the old self-definition tries to re-enter. That moment becomes a crossroad. Will you respond from the restored image, or will you retreat into the familiar version of yourself? Release means you make a decision before those moments arrive: *I will no longer return to who I used to be for comfort.*

This is why God speaks so strongly in Isaiah—not because He is insensitive to the past, but because He is committed to the future. The next verse reveals His intention: *"Behold, I will do a new thing; now it shall spring forth." Isaiah 43:19*

New things cannot fully spring forth where the heart keeps returning to old references. The old image may feel familiar, but familiarity is not freedom. The past may feel known, but known is not always safe. Many believers return to old patterns because the unknown requires faith, while the old image requires only memory. But permanence is built when faith replaces memory as the guiding force.

Release is how you honor what God has done. It is how you say, "This healing is real, and I will live as though it is." It is how you protect your future from the pull of old definitions. The old image does not disappear because time passes. It loses power because agreement ends. And when agreement ends, permanence begins.

Why the Old Image Tries to Follow You
The old image often attempts to follow the believer into new seasons—not because it still holds authority, but because familiarity feels safe. The old image is a *learned identity*. It was formed through repeated experiences, reinforced through survival patterns, and protected through emotional habits. Even after healing, the mind and emotions may still recognize the old image as "normal," simply because it has been

practiced for years. This is why old thought patterns, emotional responses, and self-definitions often return during **pressure, fatigue, or transition.** Not because restoration was false, but because transition exposes what is still being retrained. The old image becomes loudest when the believer feels vulnerable—when the heart is tired, when the outcome is uncertain, when the future is unfamiliar, or when something triggers a memory of past pain. This does not mean failure. It reveals that release is a process requiring intention. Healing restores truth, but the mind must learn to *live from it* consistently. Old images do not always depart through one revelation; they fade as the believer stops agreeing with them.

Often, the old image follows you in subtle ways:
1) Familiarity feels like safety.
The old identity may be painful, but it is predictable. The new identity may be healed, but it may feel unfamiliar. This is why some believers unconsciously return to old thinking—not because they want bondage, but because unfamiliar freedom requires faith. Familiar pain can feel safer than unfamiliar wholeness.
2) The mind reaches for what it has rehearsed.
Under stress, the mind often defaults to what it practiced most. If anxiety was rehearsed for years,

anxiety may reappear when pressure rises. If self-doubt was once a constant companion, it may try to speak again when you step into new responsibility. The old image returns because it was once reinforced through repetition. Scripture speaks to this principle clearly: *"Be not conformed to this world: but be ye transformed by the renewing of your mind." Romans 12:2* Renewal is necessary because old patterns do not disappear automatically—they must be replaced.

3) Old triggers attempt to reopen old agreements. Sometimes the old image returns because something resembles the past—tone of voice, rejection, delay, betrayal, being misunderstood. The enemy often uses triggers to invite the believer back into old narratives: *See? Nothing has changed. You're still the same. This is how it always ends.* But triggers are invitations, not commands. They only gain power when agreement is renewed.

4) Transition exposes what is still being healed. New seasons are stretching seasons. They require new thinking, new responses, and new confidence. The old image often follows because transition tests identity. When stepping into something new—greater responsibility, deeper calling, higher visibility, new relationships—the old image attempts to reassert itself so the believer retreats into what feels manageable. This is why Jesus warned against divided focus: *"No man, having put his hand to the plough, and looking back, is fit for the kingdom of God." Luke 9:62*

Looking back does not mean abandoning faith—it means **dividing focus**. A person may still love God, still worship, still pray, yet keep referencing the old self-definition as a safety net. The plough represents forward movement and building. Looking back interrupts progress because the heart becomes split between the past and the future.

Permanence requires **forward agreement**. It requires deciding that the old image will no longer be your reference point. When the old identity tries to follow you, the response is not panic—it is discernment. You recognize the voice, refuse the agreement, and return to what God has revealed. Scripture gives language for this intentional forward posture: *"Forgetting those things which are behind, and reaching forth unto those things which are before." Philippians 3:13* Forgetting here is not erasing memory—it is removing authority. The old image tries to follow because it was once familiar. But familiarity is not freedom. The old voice may return, but it does not have to be obeyed. It can knock—but it does not have to enter. And every time you refuse to look back, you strengthen permanence.

The Danger of Keeping Old Labels

Old images often survive through old labels. Words such as *broken, overlooked, insecure, unworthy,* or *always struggling* may once have described a season of pain, but they no longer serve truth. When these labels are carried forward, they quietly reopen agreements that God has already healed.

Labels shape language, and language reinforces identity. What you repeatedly call yourself becomes what you unconsciously live from. Even when healing has begun, continuing to use old identifiers can tether the soul to a version of self that no longer exists. Scripture addresses this directly: *"That ye put off concerning the former conversation the old man."* Ephesians 4:22

Putting off is not automatic; it is intentional. It requires awareness and decision. The old image does not disappear simply because truth has been revealed—it must be deliberately released. Healing makes release possible, but agreement completes it. God does not restore a person so they can continue speaking from past distortion. He restores so that identity, language, and alignment can come into agreement. When old labels remain, they subtly resist permanence. When they are released, freedom deepens.

Letting go of old labels is not denial of what was endured; it is discernment about what no longer defines you. What once explained pain must not be allowed to explain purpose.

Lot's Wife: When the Old Image Is Not Released
Scripture gives a sobering example of what happens when the old image is not fully released. **Lot's wife** physically left Sodom, but inwardly she remained attached to what she was asked to abandon. *"But his wife looked back from behind him, and she became a pillar of salt." Genesis 19:26*

Looking back was not curiosity—it was attachment. She obeyed the instruction to leave, but she did not complete the act of release. Her body moved forward, yet her identity remained tethered to what had shaped her. The old image still held authority. This moment reveals a profound truth: **deliverance without release produces immobility**. She escaped the place, but not the internal agreement formed there. The past was no longer her location, but it was still her reference point.

This account is not centered on punishment; it is centered on permanence. What is not released cannot be escaped. What is carried forward eventually stops progress. The soul cannot move freely into what God is establishing while still looking back to what He has redeemed.

Lot's wife reminds us that transition requires more than movement—it requires agreement. God may remove you from an environment, but only surrender releases the identity that environment shaped. Freedom is not only about where you go; it is about what you let go of. When the old image is not released, it competes with the new one God is forming. And where there is competition, progress stalls. This is why release is not optional. It is the final act that allows restoration to become permanent.

Leaving Without Resentment
Leaving the old image behind does not require bitterness toward the past. Healing does not rewrite history; it redeems meaning. You can honor what you survived without allowing it to define who you are now. Release is not denial—it is discernment.

Resentment keeps the past active. It ties identity to injury and keeps memory in a position of authority.

When resentment remains, the old image lingers—not because it is true, but because it is still being referenced. True freedom comes when the past is acknowledged but no longer consulted. Scripture captures this posture with clarity: *"Forgetting those things which are behind, and reaching forth unto those things which are before." Philippians 3:13*

Forgetting here does not mean erasing memory—it means removing authority. It is the decision to stop drawing identity from what has already been redeemed. The past may explain where you have been, but it no longer determines where you are going. Leaving without resentment allows the heart to move forward without carrying unnecessary weight. Gratitude replaces bitterness. Wisdom replaces regret. The soul learns to remember without returning and to acknowledge without reliving. This posture protects progress. It keeps the believer from defining themselves by what they endured rather than by what God has restored. When resentment is released, movement becomes lighter, clarity becomes sharper, and identity settles more fully into truth.

You do not have to resent the past to leave it. You only have to stop letting it speak.

Agreeing Fully with Who God Says You Are

The final step of release is agreement. Restoration reveals the true image, but agreement is what establishes it. The believer must fully agree with what God has spoken—even when emotions lag behind truth. Agreement is not denial of feeling; it is the decision to place truth above feeling. Scripture frames this clearly: *"Let God be true, but every man a liar." Romans 3:4*

This is not a statement of confrontation; it is a declaration of authority. When God's truth becomes the highest reference point, every competing voice loses credibility. The old image may attempt to resurface through memory, emotion, or habit, but it no longer holds jurisdiction.

Agreement solidifies identity. It moves truth from revelation into residence. What God has revealed must be believed, embraced, and lived from—not occasionally revisited, but fully inhabited. Leaving the old image behind means:
- You stop introducing yourself through pain instead of purpose.
- You stop rehearsing explanations God has already healed.

- You stop expecting outcomes based on former limitations.
- You stop shrinking to feel safe when God has called you to stand.

Agreement is the moment identity stops being debated internally. The believer no longer negotiates with past definitions or waits for emotional confirmation. Truth is accepted because God has spoken it. This is where permanence is formed. When agreement is complete, the old image no longer follows—it has nowhere to attach. Identity becomes settled, language becomes aligned, and life begins to flow from truth rather than memory. Agreement is not arrogance. It is obedience. And when the believer agrees fully with who God says they are, release is no longer fragile—it is final.

Living Forward Without Negotiation
Once the old image is released, life begins to simplify. Decisions gain clarity. Obedience becomes steadier. The internal conflict between who you were and who God says you are dissolves. Identity is no longer debated; it is inhabited. Scripture confirms this forward posture with unmistakable finality: *"Therefore if any man be in Christ, he is a new creature: old things are*

passed away; behold, all things are become new." 2 Corinthians 5:17

Newness here is not partial. It is complete. It does not require repeated renegotiation or constant reaffirmation. When God declares something new, it is established—not provisional.

Living forward without negotiation means the believer stops revisiting old definitions during moments of pressure. The past is no longer consulted for guidance, explanation, or validation. Memory may remain, but authority does not. This posture produces freedom. Life is no longer managed through self-protection, over-explanation, or fear of regression. The believer moves forward from truth, not reaction. They obey without bargaining, trust without reservation, and stand without apology.

Negotiation ends where agreement begins. When identity is settled, direction follows naturally. The soul rests—not because challenges disappear, but because the question of *who am I* has already been answered. Living forward is not about striving to become someone else. It is about remaining aligned with who God has already declared you to be. And when identity is no longer negotiated, progress becomes inevitable.

Prayer: Releasing the Old Image
Father,
I thank You for restoring my identity and revealing truth. Today, I release every old image that no longer agrees with Your Word. I let go of former labels, former limitations, and former narratives. I choose to live forward—fully aligned with who You say I am. Establish permanence in my heart. Let no old agreement regain authority, and let truth remain my reference point in every season. I receive the identity You have restored and commit to living from it without hesitation or retreat. In Jesus' name, Amen.

What you fully release can no longer define you, and what God has restored now stands without competition.

Chapter Fourteen
Established in the Image

From Transformation to Permanence

Restoration begins a journey. Alignment shapes a lifestyle. Release removes what no longer belongs. But **establishment** is what makes the work permanent. This chapter is not about becoming—it is about **being**. It marks the point where identity is no longer fragile, transitional, or questioned. The image God revealed is now rooted.

Many believers live between transformation and permanence. They have encountered God genuinely, yet they keep revisiting who they are. Each challenge forces a reassessment. Each delay triggers self-examination. Each opposition reopens old questions. Establishment ends this cycle.

To be established means the believer no longer lives in cycles of rediscovery. There is no repeated need to revisit identity every time pressure arises. Identity has settled. The soul has agreed. Life now flows from a place of **internal stability rather than constant self-evaluation**. Scripture speaks to this grounding with clarity: *"Rooted and built up in him, and stablished in the faith." Colossians 2:7*

Establishment is not emotional confidence; it is **spiritual anchoring**. It is being rooted deeply enough that storms no longer uproot identity. The winds may blow, but the foundation does not move. The transformation of **Paul** offers one of the clearest biblical pictures of this transition from encounter to permanence.

Before he was Paul, he was Saul—moving with certainty, conviction, and authority, yet completely misaligned. Saul was not confused about who he was; he was wrong about **what he was living from**. His identity was anchored in zeal without revelation. *"And Saul, yet breathing out threatenings and slaughter against the disciples of the Lord…" Acts 9:1*

On the road to persecute Christians, Saul encountered Christ. In a moment, revelation shattered distortion. *"Saul, Saul, why persecutest thou me?" Acts 9:4*

That encounter was transformational—but notice something important: **it was not yet establishment**. After the encounter, Saul was blind, silent, and waiting. His former identity was broken, but his new identity had not yet been fully rooted. This season mattered. God did not rush Saul into public ministry immediately. He allowed time for **alignment and anchoring**. Later, Scripture records a crucial shift: *"But Saul increased the more in strength, and confounded the Jews…"* Acts 9:22

This was not just growth in boldness—it was **establishment**. Saul no longer wavered between who he was and who he had been. He did not keep referencing his former life as a qualifier. He no longer negotiated identity under pressure. He lived from what God had revealed.

Eventually, Saul became Paul—not merely in name, but in **permanence**. He did not return to his old image during persecution, imprisonment, rejection, or suffering. His identity remained anchored even when circumstances were violent and unpredictable. *"I know whom I have believed."* 2 Timothy 1:12 That statement is the voice of establishment.

Paul did not say, *"I am discovering who I am."* He said, *"I know."* This is the difference between transformation and permanence. Transformation changes direction. Establishment **secures it**.

An established believer does not re-evaluate identity under pressure. They do not reinterpret calling when challenged. They do not retreat into old definitions when suffering arises. They remain rooted. Scripture affirms this maturity: *"That we henceforth be no more children, tossed to and fro." Ephesians 4:14*

Establishment produces steadiness. It removes spiritual instability. The believer no longer swings between confidence and doubt, boldness and fear, clarity and confusion. When identity is established:
- Faith is steady, not seasonal
- Obedience is consistent, not emotional
- Confidence is quiet, not performative

This is the place where the mirror no longer needs constant adjustment. The image is clear. The foundation is firm. The work is permanent. Establishment does not mean the journey ends. It means **identity no longer interrupts it.**

When Identity No Longer Wavers
An established identity does not mean life becomes easy; it means life becomes **clear**. The person may still encounter opposition, delay, misunderstanding, or transition, but these no longer shake the foundation. Challenges no longer provoke panic because identity is not fragile. Decisions are made from truth rather than reaction. Faith is exercised

with confidence rather than anxiety. Scripture describes this steadiness with precision: *"That we henceforth be no more children, tossed to and fro." Ephesians 4:14*

Spiritual maturity brings stability. The person is no longer governed by every opinion, emotion, or circumstance. Identity remains consistent across seasons—whether in favor or opposition, abundance or limitation. This consistency is evidence that identity has moved from discovery to establishment.

The life of **Joseph** illustrates this unwavering identity clearly. Joseph's life changed repeatedly and dramatically. He moved from favored son to betrayed brother, from slave to prisoner, and eventually from prisoner to ruler. Yet across every season, Joseph's identity remained intact.

When Joseph was sold into slavery, his environment changed—but his character did not. When he was falsely accused and imprisoned, his circumstances shifted—but his integrity remained. Joseph did not redefine himself by betrayal, injustice, or delay. He continued to live from the identity God had revealed through his early dreams. *"The Lord was with Joseph." Genesis 39:21*

This statement appears repeatedly in Scripture—not because Joseph's life was easy, but because his identity was anchored. Joseph did not react to pain by abandoning who he was. He did not compromise his values to escape difficulty. He remained consistent when no one was watching and faithful when no reward was visible.

Later, when Joseph stood before Pharaoh, he did not shrink because of his past, nor did he boast because of his position. His identity was steady. *"It is not in me: God shall give Pharaoh an answer of peace."* Genesis 41:16

This is the language of an established identity. Joseph did not need to prove himself or protect himself. He lived from clarity, not insecurity.

When identity no longer wavers, responses change. The believer does not overreact to criticism or collapse under pressure. They remain anchored. They listen, discern, and respond from alignment rather than impulse. This is the point where the mirror no longer needs constant adjustment. The reflection is clear—and it remains so. The believer no longer asks, *"Who am I now?"* every time circumstances change. Identity is not redefined by seasons; it **outlasts** them. Scripture affirms this kind of grounding: *"Being confident of this very thing, that he which hath begun a good work in you will perform it." Philippians 1:6*

Confidence here is not emotional—it is settled assurance. It is the quiet strength that comes from knowing God has completed the foundation.
When identity no longer wavers:
- Faith remains steady under pressure
- Obedience remains consistent in delay
- Peace remains present in uncertainty

This is maturity. This is establishment. This is living from truth without interruption. And when identity is this secure, life no longer feels unstable—it feels **directed**.

Living Established, Not Defensive
When identity is not established, believers often live defensively. They explain themselves too much. They anticipate rejection before it happens. They brace for disappointment, criticism, or misunderstanding. Words are chosen carefully out of fear, and decisions are delayed out of insecurity. Life is lived in a guarded posture.

But establishment removes defensiveness. When identity is settled, there is no longer a need to protect who you are—because who you are is secure. The believer no longer reacts to opposition as a threat to self-worth. Truth no longer feels fragile. Scripture confirms this peace-filled confidence: *"The Lord is my light and my salvation; whom shall I fear?" Psalm 27:1*

Fear loses its influence when identity is settled. The believer is no longer driven by the need to guard themselves constantly. Trust replaces tension. Confidence becomes quiet, not combative. The heart remains open without becoming vulnerable to distortion. Living established also means the believer stops shrinking during challenge. They do not retreat into silence out of fear, nor do they overcompensate with force to prove strength. They remain present, grounded, and calm—able to stand without striving.

The life of **Nehemiah** demonstrates this posture clearly. Nehemiah was called to rebuild the walls of Jerusalem—a visible, public assignment that attracted criticism, mockery, and intimidation. His leadership was constantly challenged. *"But it came to pass, that when Sanballat heard that we builded the wall, he was wroth, and took great indignation." Nehemiah 4:1*

Nehemiah faced accusations questioning his motives, competence, and authority. Yet notice his response: he did not over-explain himself. He did not abandon the work to defend his reputation. He did not react emotionally to mockery. Instead, Nehemiah stayed focused and anchored. *"So built we the wall… for the people had a mind to work."* Nehemiah 4:6

This is the posture of an established identity. Nehemiah did not need external validation to continue. His confidence came from calling, not approval. Even when enemies attempted to distract him with false concern, he responded with clarity rather than defensiveness. *"I am doing a great work, so that I cannot come down."* Nehemiah 6:3

This statement reveals identity without arrogance. Nehemiah did not justify himself; he simply stayed aligned. He trusted God's assignment more than he feared people's opinions.

Living established frees the believer from the exhausting need to manage perception. When identity is secure, silence can be strong. Presence can be enough. The believer does not need to win every argument or correct every misunderstanding.

Scripture affirms this settled confidence: *"Commit thy way unto the Lord; trust also in him; and he shall bring it to pass." Psalm 37:5*

Trust allows God to defend what no longer needs defending. When identity is established, the believer rests in God's ability to vindicate.

Living established does not mean living detached. It means living **anchored**. The heart remains soft without becoming fearful. The posture remains open without becoming unstable.

Defensiveness fades where identity is secure. Reaction gives way to discernment. Tension gives way to trust. And when a believer lives established, life is no longer navigated from fear of being misunderstood—but from confidence in being aligned. That is freedom with maturity.

Established Faith Produces Endurance
Establishment produces endurance. When identity and faith are settled, the believer learns how to remain faithful without constant affirmation or immediate results. Obedience becomes steady rather than seasonal. Faith is no longer driven by emotion,

applause, or urgency. Waiting no longer threatens confidence, because confidence is no longer tied to speed. Scripture affirms this kind of endurance: *"Cast not away therefore your confidence, which hath great recompence of reward." Hebrews 10:35*

The confidence spoken of here is not boldness or outward enthusiasm. It is **assurance**—a quiet knowing that what God has spoken is settled, even when fulfillment unfolds slowly. Established faith does not need frequent reassurance. It trusts the integrity of God's Word.

Endurance is the fruit of establishment. When faith is not yet rooted, delay feels like rejection. Silence feels like absence. Waiting feels like loss. But when faith is established, delay is understood as process rather than denial. The believer no longer interprets time as opposition. An established believer does not abandon truth because of delay. They understand that **timing does not cancel identity**. God's promises do not expire because fulfillment requires patience.

The life of **Noah** illustrates this endurance powerfully. Noah received a word from God that contradicted his environment, culture, and experience. He was instructed to build an ark for a flood that had never been seen. *"Thus did Noah; according to all that God commanded him, so did he."* Genesis 6:22

Notice that Scripture does not describe Noah questioning the length of time or seeking repeated confirmation. Noah's faith was established in God's voice. He built consistently, year after year, without visible evidence, public support, or immediate reward. Noah endured mockery, misunderstanding, and isolation—not because he was emotionally strong, but because his faith was anchored. He did not need rain to validate obedience. He trusted God's word enough to keep building in silence.

This is the nature of established faith. It continues working when results are delayed. It obeys when affirmation is absent. It trusts when evidence is invisible. Scripture reinforces this principle: *"For ye have need of patience, that, after ye have done the will of God, ye might receive the promise."* Hebrews 10:36

Endurance is not passive waiting; it is **active faithfulness over time**. Established believers understand that obedience precedes fulfillment, and patience protects promise.

When faith is established, the believer no longer rushes God. They do not compromise to accelerate outcomes. They remain faithful, knowing that God is faithful. *"Let us not be weary in well doing: for in due season we shall reap, if we faint not." Galatians 6:9*

Endurance keeps the believer from fainting. It allows faith to outlast frustration. It anchors obedience when emotions fluctuate.

Established faith produces endurance because it rests in agreement. The believer no longer wonders if God will do what He said. They know He will—*when the time is right*. Delay does not weaken established faith. It **proves** it. And when endurance is complete, fulfillment arrives without eroding identity. That is the strength of a faith that is established.

Established to Reflect Christ Consistently

The final fruit of establishment is **consistency**. When identity is fully rooted, the believer no longer reflects Christ only in certain moments, moods, or environments. Christlikeness is no longer situational. The image remains evident across seasons—quietly, faithfully, and without effort.

Consistency is not perfection. It is **alignment sustained over time**. It is the ability to respond with grace under pressure, to remain faithful in obscurity, and to walk steadily whether seen or unseen. Established believers no longer fluctuate between spiritual intensity and emotional withdrawal. Their lives reflect Christ because their identity is no longer fragmented. Scripture describes this lasting work with assurance: *"Being confident of this very thing, that he which hath begun a good work in you will perform it." Philippians 1:6*

God completes what He begins. Establishment is evidence that the work has reached maturity—not that the believer has arrived at perfection, but that the foundation has been secured. The believer is no longer rebuilding what God has already finished.

When establishment is present, the believer no longer lives as someone *becoming* healed, *becoming* aligned, or *becoming* whole. They live as someone **established**—secure in identity, steady in faith, and anchored in truth. Their spiritual life is no longer episodic. It is consistent.

The life of **Barnabas** offers a clear picture of this consistency. Barnabas was not the most visible apostle, nor the loudest voice in the early church. Yet Scripture consistently describes him as a man whose life reflected Christ through encouragement, faithfulness, and discernment. *"For he was a good man, and full of the Holy Ghost and of faith." Acts 11:24*

Notice the language—*good man, full, faith*. This was not a momentary description; it was a reputation formed over time. Barnabas did not reflect Christ only when things were going well. He remained steady when others doubted, feared, or withdrew. When Saul (later Paul) was newly converted and mistrusted by the church, it was Barnabas who stood with him. *"But Barnabas took him, and brought him to the apostles." Acts 9:27*

This act reveals consistent Christlikeness. Barnabas was not swayed by fear or public opinion. He lived from an established identity that allowed him to discern, encourage, and stand firm in truth. Later, when John Mark failed during ministry, Barnabas again demonstrated consistency—not by abandoning truth, but by extending grace and believing in restoration. *"And Barnabas determined to take with them John." Acts 15:37*

Barnabas reflected Christ not through dramatic moments, but through **repeated faithfulness**. His life carried the same tone across seasons: encouragement, steadiness, and trust in God's work in others. This is what it means to be established enough to reflect Christ consistently. The believer does not change spiritual posture based on environment. They are the same in private as in public, in waiting as in fulfillment, in obscurity as in visibility. Scripture affirms this mature consistency: *"Jesus Christ the same yesterday, and to day, and for ever."* Hebrews 13:8

As believers mature, their lives begin to mirror this steadiness—not because they are Christ, but because they are **established in Him**. Consistency becomes their testimony. Not loud declarations, but faithful presence. Not emotional highs, but steady obedience. Not occasional reflection, but continual alignment. Established believers reflect Christ because they are no longer striving to resemble Him. They are living from the image He has already formed. And when reflection becomes consistent, the life itself becomes a witness—quietly revealing the faithfulness of the God who finishes what He begins.

A Life That Does Not Return

Establishment means there is **no return to the former image**. No revisiting old definitions. No renegotiating identity under pressure. No allowing the past to compete with truth. What once explained you no longer defines you. What once shaped you no longer speaks with authority. This is not denial of history—it is **finality of direction**. Scripture declares this with unmistakable clarity: *"If any man be in Christ, he is a new creature: old things are passed away; behold, all things are become new."* 2 Corinthians 5:17

Newness here is not temporary. It is not seasonal. It is not conditional. It is **permanent**. The old image does not linger as an option. It no longer has voting rights in the believer's identity.

A life that does not return is not lived in fear of relapse. It is lived in **confidence of establishment**. The believer no longer guards identity anxiously. Identity feels solid—something to stand upon, not something to protect constantly.

The life of **Ruth** offers a powerful picture of this kind of finality. Ruth did not simply leave Moab geographically; she left it **internally**. Her declaration was not emotional—it was permanent alignment.

Whither thou goest, I will go... thy people shall be my people, and thy God my God." Ruth 1:16

Ruth did not return to her former land, former gods, or former identity—even when life remained uncertain. She did not keep Moab as a fallback option. Her new direction was not cautious; it was committed. Because she did not look back, she was positioned to move forward into redemption, provision, and legacy. A life that does not return understands this truth: **forward agreement unlocks future inheritance.**

The prophet **Elisha** provides another striking example. When Elisha was called, he did not keep the tools of his former life as security. He destroyed them. *"And he took the yoke of oxen, and slew them... and followed Elijah." 1 Kings 19:21*

Elisha did not burn the plow out of anger toward his past. He did it to eliminate retreat. His action declared, *I am not going back.* The former life was not evil—it was simply no longer aligned. This is what establishment looks like in practice. The believer does not keep old identities, habits, or narratives as emotional safety nets. They do not return to old definitions during disappointment or pressure. They do not speak from former pain when challenged. Scripture reinforces this forward posture: *"No man, having put his hand to the plough, and looking back, is fit for the kingdom of God." Luke 9:62*

Looking back does not mean remembering—it means **reconsidering**. A life that does not return refuses reconsideration. Identity has been settled. The believer now lives forward—not anxiously, not cautiously, but confidently. Decisions are no longer filtered through former fear. Reactions are no longer shaped by old wounds. Identity no longer feels fragile or negotiable. This is not arrogance. It is agreement. A life that does not return understands:
- Healing is complete enough to be trusted.
- Truth is strong enough to be lived from.
- Identity is secure enough to remain unchanged under pressure.

The past no longer competes with truth because truth has been fully received. When establishment is complete, the believer does not say, *"I hope I don't go back."* They live as someone who **has nowhere to go back to**. The old image is not resisted—it is irrelevant. The former self is not fought—it is finished. And when identity is this established, life moves forward with clarity, peace, and authority—

not because the past was erased, but because it no longer leads.

Prayer: Established in the Image
Father,
I thank You for completing what You began in me. I receive the identity You have revealed, healed, aligned, and secured. I choose to live established—rooted in truth, anchored in faith, and confident in who I am in You. Let no former image regain influence. Let my life reflect Christ with consistency and peace. I stand in what You have spoken. In Jesus' name, Amen.

When you are established in the image God revealed, the mirror no longer asks questions—it simply reflects truth.

A Final Word to the Reader

If you have reached this point, something within you has already shifted.

This book was not written to convince you of a belief system. It was written to return you to yourself—to the truest version of who you are beneath fear, pain, survival, labels, and distortion. Whether you arrived here with faith, doubt, questions, or quiet hope, the journey you have taken is valid.

Transformation does not begin with belief. It begins with **recognition**. You have seen yourself more clearly. You have recognized patterns that no longer serve you. You have encountered truth—not as pressure, but as clarity. What you have discovered is this: You were never meant to live fragmented, defensive, or diminished. The image you now see is not something you must strive to maintain. It is something you are invited to **live from**.

From this point forward, you are no longer required to revisit who you were to explain who you are. You do not need to renegotiate your worth in moments of pressure. You do not need to shrink to feel safe or perform to feel accepted.

Living from the true image means you make decisions from alignment rather than reaction. It means you respond instead of retreat. It means you walk forward without apology for growth. This is your commission: Live from what has been revealed. Stand on what has been restored. Refuse to return to old definitions when life becomes uncomfortable.

You are not responsible for convincing others of who you are. You are responsible for **being** who you are. Let your life move forward from clarity. Let your words reflect truth. Let your presence carry peace.

Whether your faith is strong, emerging, or still forming, you have permission to live whole. You are allowed to grow without explanation. You are allowed to change without guilt. You are allowed to live from truth without fear of losing yourself—because yourself has been found.

This is not the end of a book. It is the beginning of a posture. May you live established. May you remain aligned. May the image you now see guide you forward—quietly, confidently, and without return.

A Sealing Prayer for You

Take a moment. Breathe. Let what you have read settle—not in your emotions, but in your understanding.

This prayer is for **you**—not for who you used to be, not for who you are trying to become, but for who you are **now**, standing in clarity. May what has been revealed to you remain steady. May what has been restored within you stay intact. May the image you now see no longer feel fragile or temporary.

I speak peace over your inner life. Not the kind of peace that ignores reality, but the kind that steadies you within it. May confusion lose its voice. May old narratives lose their authority. May clarity become familiar. May you trust what you now know about yourself. May you stop questioning what has already been healed. May you move forward without carrying explanations you no longer owe.

If faith is part of your language, may you know that God completes what He begins. If faith is still forming, may truth continue to meet you gently and honestly. Either way, may wholeness remain your posture.

I pray that when pressure comes, you do not return to old definitions. That when delay appears, you do not doubt what has been established. That when uncertainty arises, you respond from alignment rather than fear. May your decisions be made from truth, not urgency. May your voice reflect confidence, not defense. May your presence carry calm, not tension. You are not required to prove your growth. You are not required to revisit your pain. You are not required to shrink for comfort. May your life now move forward from a settled place. May the image you see guide how you speak, choose, love, and lead. May you live from what is true—quietly, consistently, and without return.

This work within you is sealed. What has been restored is now established. What has been revealed is now yours to live from. Amen.

About the Author

Racheal Odoy is a writer and speaker whose work centers on identity, clarity, and inner restoration. She is known for guiding people through honest reflection—helping them recognize how life experiences shape self-perception and how truth restores wholeness. Her writing is grounded, reflective, and accessible, drawing from years of working with individuals navigating personal growth, transition, and healing. Racheal writes for readers across backgrounds and belief systems, offering insight that invites reflection, personal responsibility, and freedom. Her work speaks to those who appear strong outwardly yet seek alignment and stability within.

www.ingramcontent.com/pod-product-compliance
Lightning Source LLC
Chambersburg PA
CBHW070637160426
43194CB00009B/1481